The Same Sun Over All

Jeff Vinter

Jeff Vinter was born in Lambeth in 1953 and educated at Chichester, Exeter and Winchester. In 1969, he started to write lyrics for a Sussex folk group, moving on to free verse in the 1970s before returning to more traditional forms in the mid 1980s.

This collection includes revisions to many earlier works, as well as some entirely new pieces written in the last few years. The dates of composition and, where appropriate, revision are included, together with some explanatory notes at the end.

The Same Sun Over All

Collected Lyrics and Poems
1969 – 2010

Jeff Vinter

Crosswave Publishing

First published in 2010

Crosswave Publishing
1 Victoria Road
Chichester
West Sussex
PO19 7HY

ISBN 978-0-9565561-0-3

Set in Dauphin, Georgia and Tahoma

Printed in Great Britain by Imprint Digital (imprintdigital.net)

For Rosie and Heather

'I shall not be the commercial type of ghost,
Pointing to boxes of gold under the floor
And certainly I don't intend to jangle chains
Or carry my head ... (such a gruesome type of chore).

'I shall not cause draughts, be noisy, spoil your "let", –
In fact, to be brief, I shan't materialise.
But I shall be pleased if anyone ever sees me
In your face or walk or the glance of your laughing eyes.'

from 'To a Descendent'
Lorna Wood

Acknowledgements

I am indebted to Francis Bassett, John and Sally Fisher, Phil Ridgway, Martin Vinter, Cheryl Vivian, and Janice and Rod White for their long term encouragement and support. I am also grateful to members of the Chichester Stanza, especially Andrew Bailey, Melanie Penycate and Adam Taylor, for their many constructive suggestions.

A number of these poems have been published previously:
Anchor Books: Fizzy Feet
Arundel Brewery (www.arundelbrewery.co.uk): The Twelve Drays of Christmas
'Beyond the Pale' (www.procolharum.com): Tornado Torment
Candelabrum: A Cornish Lament, Cleeve Abbey, Flame, In a Sussex Lane, Mapping the Past, Powerstock, Stogumber Station, The Winchester Diver
Forward Press: Night Lines at Bursledon Station, The Keeper of the Tower
Martlit: After the Battle, Alfie Wonders
Mosaic: Honeysuckle
Railway Ramblings: A Cornish Lament, Ghost Train, Owencarrow Viaduct, The Train Cometh Not
Rubies in the Darkness: Generations, Lost, Mantra, Radio Days
The Abbey Chronicle: Cleeve Abbey
The Poetry Church (magazine and anthologies): A Small Forgotten Door, Advent Sneaks In, At the School of Monetary Art, Christmas Pays, Credo, Eat What You Kill, In a Sussex Lane, In Your Darkest Hour, Nails, Prayer, The Gift, Travelling Blind, Who Will Make the Water Clean?
The South Bank Centre Poetry Library: Cleeve Abbey, Flame, Powerstock, Stogumber Station, The Winchester Diver
The Spectator: Cleeve Abbey, Silent Wires, Stogumber Station

Fifty Years On won first prize in The Paddon Award at the University of Exeter in 2005. Lost, Till Easter Dawns Again and Winter achieved top ten listings in annual open poetry competitions run by 'Rubies in the Darkness' in 2007 and 2009.

The cover illustration was created by manipulating copyright-free images from morgueFile (www.morguefile.com).

Contents

Echo

In the dark of falling evening
in this quiet and empty place,
I will sit here in the moonlight,
cast adrift in time and space.
I will watch the white waves breaking,
spilling softly on the shore,
and as the night enfolds me
I will dream of you once more.

How bright the lights were shining
on the road that led from here.
I still make believe I'm happy
and pretend my path is clear,
but though perhaps I'm smiling,
I am smiling on my own:
in the echo of your laughter
is the love I might have known.

1969, 1979, 1998, 2002

The Castle

The crumbling old castle, forlorn on the hill,
stood shattered and slighted and cannon-scarred still,
its raw splintered walls laced with lichens and moss
where soldiers at arms used to measure their loss.

The flank of a tower still clawed at the sky,
its limestone as grey as the clouds marching by,
and grass-tangled steps climbed uneven and steep
to grieve for the stones which had once been the keep.

The road to the gatehouse still beats to a cause,
but not for a king raising gold for his wars.
Now coachloads of tourists arrayed at the tills
lay siege to the past in the pale Purbeck hills.

1969, 2003, 2010

Starlight

Pinprick stars pour out their light,
punctuate the cloak of night.
Through the lenses, still it comes.
How long since it left those suns?

Earth-bound lovers watch the sky,
find a star to promise by
constant as their hearts' intent
though its fire may all be spent.

This ancient light.
This headlong flight.
This soaring height.
This far flung night.

1969, 2007, 2010

Alfie Wonders

Alfie wonders how he'll ever last
from this week to the next one.
The clocks at work don't go too fast,
but that is not the question.
It's not that Alfie's ever found
much time for contemplation;
it's rather that he's feeling down
against his inclination.

Alfie wonders as he turns the lathe
about his *raison d'être,*
decides the matter's rather grave
and leaves the choice till later.
It's not that Alfie's ever found
the purpose that he's seeking;
he'd rather not the truth got round
of what he half-believes in.

1970

After the Battle

By a candle in the corner
in the shadows of the light
stands a feeble-minded soldier
who has lost his will to fight.
For the sight of bleeding bodies
and the thought of wasted lives
have destroyed his soldier's logic
of sabres, swords and knives.

By the cobwebs in the cupboard
where forgotten soldiers hide
lies a broken suit of armour
that has fallen on its side.
For its fighting days are over
and the sword shall strike no more
on the armour of a stranger
in a proud and distant war.

As he walks away he's crying
for a cause he does not trust,
for the cost of soldiers dying
doesn't make the conflict just.
And the day is surely coming
when all soldiers know as he
that greed is all the battle
and death, the victory.

1970

The Autumn Wind

Have you seen the colours changing,
falling into red and gold?
Have you seen life rearranging?

Have you seen the swallows flying,
stealing from the fading sky?
Have you seen the late buds dying?

Have you seen the cloak of evening,
settling like an ashen shroud?
Have you seen the willows weeping?

Footsteps crackle in the lifeless firs;
dead leaves rattle as a cold wind stirs.

1970, 1979, 2006, 2010

Klok

Klok stands
tick tock
making funny noises
creaking hands
oil cans
old clockwork poises
ratchets winding
cracked bells chiming
dull and dusty clanks
gear wheels grating
chromium plating
rusted metal cranks

Tick tock tick tock
wish that it would stop
tick tock tick tock
wish that it would stop

Klok stands
tick tock
counting out forever
loaded coil
strain and toil
no silence ever
agitation
levitation
launched through time and space
arc descending
steel case bending
skyward staring face

Tick tock tick tock
still it doesn't stop
cheap crock cheap crock
still it doesn't

1970, 2006, 2010

Just An Illusion

I went to the preacher
and smiling with glee
said 'God's an illusion,
don't you agree?'
I told him the deaths
from a number of wars,
showed him the slaughter
forgetting the cause.

I went to the surgeon
and showed him the pain,
said 'See the misery,
can you explain?'
I told him that some
found it hard to endure,
showed him the illness
forgetting the cure.

I went to the preacher
who smiling with glee
said 'God's ways are strange,
don't you agree?'
I went to the graveyard
and feeling quite small
decided the preacher
was right after all.

1971

Falling Leaves in Autumn

As the slow world's solemn turning
makes the sallow daylight fade
and the last insistent flowers
curl and wither in the shade
the falling leaves of autumn
spiral softly through the glade

As the stone walls sink and slumber
in a glaze of frozen moss
and the pathways through the forest
gain a sheen of icy gloss
the falling leaves of autumn
weave a carpet from their loss

As the woodland turns to winter
and the days of ice begin
with the drying of the knuckles
and the cracking of the skin
the fallen leaves of autumn
stir like ashes in the wind

1971, 2010

Old Ways and Schooldays

The old town was still as it stood in the sunset.
Long shadows lengthened and slowly crept on.
Shop windows peeped out on empty grey pavements.
Softly the colours of daylight were gone.

And so through the half-light of cold autumn evening,
we wandered alone through the parts of the town;
through backstreets and backyards and old rusty footpaths
with time on our hands until darkness came down.

And there by a trainyard we talked of old summers,
alone in the silence of grey narrow streets;
laughing, remembering old ways and schooldays,
looking for somewhere to buy a few sweets.

1971

Aftersong

As the sun begins to settle
in its shades of evening red,
her face reflects the beauty
of the colours overhead.
She laughs amidst the fields of wheat
(her tears have long since dried),
remembers how she cried
and wonders why I can't forget her.

In the shadows of my memory
her whispers still remain.
When the day has died of silence
I can hear her just the same.
Our promises of long ago
were more than we could live;
I'm ready to forgive
and maybe time will draw us closer.

1972

Music in the Night

Sometimes in the silence
I can hear the music of a strange and distant orchestra
ever so quietly,
eerily,
almost inaudible against the night.

All my life long
someone has been conducting this orchestra,
the artist's artist,
the creator *par excellence.*

He goes about his work most unobtrusively.
And sometimes I can hear him
softly playing
my symphony.

1973

Requiem

Fair stood the land in the bright light of morning.
Now all her sons have been killed in the fray.
Yesterday's promise has burned into ashes;
swords swung in anger have darkened the day.

The brave words that echo throughout silent valleys
will never make sense of the suffering and pain.
Green fields have died where the banners were broken.
The land has grown old where her young men were slain.

Who chose the glory of dying in battle?
Who fought a cause he believed to be right?
Some fool with a map and an army of soldiers,
planning his strategies into the night.

1973

In Your Darkest Hour

When the storm clouds gather,
I will bring you peace.
I will sing love's song
when you need release.
You will hear my call
on the evening tide.
You will feel my touch
when you need to hide.

When it all seems hopeless,
I will be your guide.
I will take my place,
ever by your side.
You will know I'm near
when your dark days call.
You will see my light
as the shadows fall.

When the omens blacken
and you're in their thrall,
I will be your shield:
I am Lord of all.
I will bring you joy
and renew your power.
I will cast out fear
in your darkest hour.

1973, 1980, 2004

February Sun

February sun
         shine your rays on me
Shake all the world from its sleepy cocoon
Don't bide your time – wake up soon
Oh please

February sun
         stir the barren tree
Signal the soil that it's time for new birth
Burn off all frost – fire cold earth
Unfreeze

February sun
         There's a deeper blue in heaven
         and a change in the air
         There's a hint of warming freedom
         though the bough is still bare

Slow and faithful friend
         shine your rays on me
Shake all the world from its sleepy cocoon
Don't bide your time – wake up soon
Oh please
    please
    please

Wake up soon

1974, 2007

Morning Landscape with Commuter

6 a.m. with bleary eyes.
Pale sun
bleaching out
thin sheets of cloud.
Faint mist.

Bird songs,
distant radios,
alarm clocks
as I walk down the street.

Perfunctory traffic lights
(no cars).
Chip wrappers,
Coca Cola tins
punctuate the gutter.

It is always the same
these early mornings,
always this curious half-world:

only the intimations of life,
only the 6 a.m. out-of-focus haze;
barren streets,
deserted playing fields,
maybe a stray dog
and some drone like me,
walking ...
to the station.

1974, 2006

Family Laughter

I know you'll be alright.
It's in the way you smile
and every time I hear your laughter
I know it's all worthwhile.

I've seen you round the town
riding on your old blue bike.
I've heard you in the bathroom
singing songs that I don't like.

And summer in the afternoon,
you're in the cornfields building hides.
Cricket in the evening. Sometimes
we've gone for train rides.

So for a while you're young.
You're priceless now and, you know, when
your troubles come, I'm with you.
Life gets harder then.

1975

Something That Does Not Change

Alone in the wilderness
dwelt the man of God,
dressed in goatskins,
feeding on locusts and honey.
And the Son of God likewise,
forty days and forty nights
alone in the same wilderness,
fought for the souls of men.

Now through that grim wilderness
journeys everyman on his life's errand:
the days are very long,
and at night, the wind blows brushwood
over the cold, parched earth.

It is always the same in such a place,
always so cold that faith grows weak.
And alone in the wilderness,
man still cries to his God
for the strength to carry on.

1975

Lethargy Blues

Another dismal evening
   sitting at the window,
staring at the rain
   and wond'ring where to go.

I guess I could spend
   an hour or two
drowning my sorrows
   in some lonely bar,
maybe join the tail end
   of a cinema queue
or make it to a friend's
   if it's not too far.

Friends are what
   I'm most thankful for.
All I've got to do
   is make it to the door.

1975

Out of the Fireglow

So here we are,
though I have to admit to not knowing
    where the time has gone.
    We've grown old
and the fire of experience
    loses its glow.
All the things we take for granted now
would have been in song a few years ago.

    Time slips by
just as distance drifts away.
    Old fires die
and we live more nearly
    towards each day.

    We all knew
that the long years would drain us of glory
    and corrupt our grace,
    but believed
that our laughter and memories
    might have been spared.
All our hopes seem very futile now:
time has destroyed every pleasure we shared.

    We've grown old
and the spark of youth grows dim.
    We've grown cold
and we huddle closer
    against the wind.

1975

Promises, Promises

A politician promises
to put the world to right
and juggles with half-fictions
till he can't tell day from night.
He stands upon the rostrum
and utters tales of paradise,
a latter day pied piper
who doesn't dare to name his price.

The mother of invention
is the lust to win the vote,
so parties conjure slogans
which their vassals learn by rote.
No promise is too tawdry,
no gilded dream too out of reach;
but when the real comes calling,
it's all like jetsam on the beach.

A politician focuses
on values we hold dear,
and pays his backroom stooges
to retell them loud and clear.
With words of sweet entrapment,
he sells the future that deceives
and, should he come to power,
will turn to dust like last year's leaves.

1975, 2007, 2010

Michael Otto

Michael Otto, up for breakfast,
crashes down a flight of stairs,
shouts HELLO in every corner,
cleans his teeth and says his prayers.

Michael Otto, home for dinner,
gobbles up his meat and greens,
disappears with jars and fishnets,
back at six for egg and beans.

Michael Otto laughs like fury,
brandishes a willow bat,
mispronounces English words
and grins like Carroll's Cheshire Cat.

1975

Introit

Tentative as I open the door,
I step quietly into the grey half-darkness.
Shafts of light penetrate the dusty air
from tall, recessed windows:
stained glass above the altar
beckons the eye;
madonnas, angels, saints
preside on walls, in windows,
stare out at me
as if demanding belief.

Inscriptions on walls,
gravestones beneath my feet:
silent commemorations of the dead.
Threadbare banners hang
like blackened gossamer lace:
motionless, as if to emphasise
the completeness of death.

I stare up at the vaults,
the crests of arms,
the statues, gargoyles, misericords;
survey the private chapels,
the rows of empty wooden pews,
the dust-speckled altar rail.

The echo of my feet resounds
like an intrusion in a tomb:
my breath disturbs the silence,
these static, decaying
remnants of the past.

1975

The Quest

The Princess was a lady
as fair as any rose,
but jilted her Prince Charming
the night he would propose.
The Prince grew melancholic,
or so the story goes,
until he found a brewer
to dissipate his woes.

He rode against the thunder
and struggled through the rain.
He drank at every tavern,
though little was his gain,
but mass-produced effusions
he treated with disdain:
no ghastly keg could ever
alleviate his pain!

A barman told him Heavy
was Scotland's finest brew,
a draught of auld tradition,
a bevvy good and true.
He took the lonely high road
his purpose to pursue,
but when he tried a sample,
his anguish only grew.

A traveller claimed that Ireland
was in a special class
and made a beery nectar
all others to surpass;
but froth and condensation
attended every glass
and, through his teeth, he muttered:
'Another one to pass!'

Returning on the ferry
he stumbled into Wales,
where Temperance had managed

to ruin all the ales.
He trod a weary pathway
through mountain glades and vales,
where breweries had vanished
for want of any sales.

He staggered to a free house
that beckoned from afar.
It drew him ever onwards
just like a guiding star,
but as he crossed the threshold
and saw the gleaming bar,
the brash dispensers told him:
'Another keg bazaar!'

He met a slick old brewer
who told a pack of lies.
'A pint of finest mild', he said,
'will quickly dry your eyes';
but as he filled his tankard
and the foam began to rise,
the Prince exclaimed in horror:
'This rubbish takes the prize!'

He tried a special bitter
which, emptied down the sink,
reacted in the U-bend
and made the kitchen stink.
He scoured a thousand highways
until he came to think
that Britain had no brewer
whose products he could drink.

At last he crossed the Arun
and quaffed a pint of ale
which soon renewed his vigour,
according to the tale.
His doleful quest was over!
He supped up by the pail,
but for that night's adventures
he ended up in jail.

So take to heart this moral,
wherever you may be,
in city, town or country
or beside the briny sea.
When love becomes affliction,
there's one sure remedy:
the Arundel elixir
that's known as ASB.

1976, 2007-2010

The Keeper of the Tower

Between the city and the water's edge
where shadows cross the sand,
the keeper of the tower
surveyed the frozen land.
There was nothing before that horizon
but endless fields of stone
and ugly splintered statues
where once green trees had grown.

Between the city and the water's edge
where time piles up the years,
he heard no childish laughter
nor shed the usual tears.
It was only the absolute stillness
that kept him rooted there
until his soul, like winter,
was deadwood: stripped and bare.

1976

The Gift

The heart of God
must be strangely lonely,
to love so much
and yet be loved so little.
And what does it mean
that we are made in His image?
To spring from love
and yet to live adrift?

What is it, pray,
that keeps God there,
that holds his timeless constancy?
There's scant reward
from loveless man.
What's there to care for?

The nature of the gift is all
that mankind finds unwanted,
like Christmas cards
in a sorting office
that come back
undelivered.

1976, 2005

Cat Nose and Holiday

House- and cat-sitting in the family home

You don't fool me,
cat nose stuffed under the gate,
pseudo-tiger pacing the kitchen floor!
I remember you, little kitten,
laughable ball of fur
falling from the tops of armchairs,
upturned white belly,
legs fingering the sky.
And now do you complain
that we have robbed you of your catness?

Silly ginger tom!
Just think of all the catfood in the larder,
the price of being uncat!
And do we all protest
about the mutilated
trounced-mouse torsos
on the lawn?
Flimsy furry toys that come apart
like balls of wool?

Oh cat! Uncat fat anticat!
Befuddled thin fatcat!
The house is under new management.

Do mandarins keep ponderous
nonsense cats in China?
(I ask questions like this
because it mystifies me so
to see you at the front door
waiting for them all
to come home.)

1976, 2009

After Hours

*Rush hour crowds in US city avoid heart
attack victim – BBC News report*

He looked like someone's grandad,
said the doctor,
a nice man with a now unsmiling face.
Collapsed right there on the sidewalk,
head turned skywards,
marbled eyes staring blindly into space.

Heart attack after office hours.
Just fell to his knees
in the thoroughfare and died.
He looked like someone's grandad,
but the passers-by
just crossed to the other side.

1976

Damascus

I have never been to Damascus
but I know of a saint
who travelled that road
after Christian blood.

I've been in Emmaeus
for seventeen years, but once I swear
I saw a tall stranger
on the road out of here.

It was a few years ago, I know,
and I was not near enough
to see the marks on his hands and feet,
but I believed him then.

Ever since, I have idled here
growing feeble.
In these latter days, I sometimes think
that Damascus might be better.

1976

Village Vespers

The trees in Chestnut Avenue
    have waved their sleepy heads
    goodnight,
the old sun disappeared
    behind rooftops.

Last thing at night,
    listen to the Radio Four
    bedtime story,
then a touch of the *avant garde*
    with deadpan Mr. Peel.

The children's voices
    are quiet now,
because all their heavy eyes
    are wrapped in sleep.

Last lights die down
    in The Rising Sun.
There goes the theme tune.
It's all lights out
    and time for bed.

1976

Nails

Nails and wood
go together.

Nails and wood
make toys and boxes.

Nails and wood
make crucifixions.

You know the story of the old wooden cross.
That was a brutal way to die.

But you have to think about it.
You have to see what the icons mean.

It was a brutal way to die.
Not just the nails, but the strain

of dead weight tearing His frame;
a murderous rite for life and time

with hatred at the heart
of its design.

O pax Romana,
inhumana!

1977, 2007

Cats Again

Cats live
behind the houses
around here.
All manner of cats.

Soft gentle cats
that stare down from the tops
of old garden sheds
with deep liquid eyes.
Lean streetfighting cats
poised for the kill
on narrow wooden fences.

All manner of cats,
as I say.

You can learn about cats
late at night
when the curtains are drawn
and your wife is in your arms.
You can appreciate
the catsymphonies of some
catStockhausen
after five hours' overtime
at the office.

These are a cat's objections
to our civilising influence.

If you want further proof,
there behind the houses
around here,
in amongst the old boots
and overturned milk bottles,
master of all he surveys:
the cat.

1977

After the Storm

The clouds have broken,
someone says.
I peer through parted curtains
at the mellow blue of heaven.
It's true.
The sky is empty now
save for a distant range
of mountain clouds,
and even they seem silver
in the softly pallid moonglow.

On earth,
the road lies cold and damp
over field and furrow,
through hill and vale
where man once set his plough
to tame the soil.

So gentle a touch as this,
a moistened breath of wind
through the all-pervading blue and silver,
seemed far too great a hope
before this peace.

And after the storm of years,
will such a peace as this descend
on my weary
hidebound bones?
And such a tranquil place
become my dwelling,
my rest at last in the purity
of that night?

1977, 2010

Doubting Thomas

Thomas,
are you there?
I want to talk
about the upper room.

Where is this place, Thomas?
It is not enough to answer:
'In your soul'.
For I too have doubt
and seek some firmer
assurance.

Are the memories
flooding back?
Can you be sure
after all these years?

Think carefully, Thomas,
for I trust you
as a man after my own
inclination.

You remember where it was?
A map, Thomas,
draw me a map!
See, I have
pencil and paper.

And the man,
yes, the man!
How did you know
it was him?
How could you be
so certain?

Oh, the wounds.
Is that all?
Even scars can be
a clever subterfuge.

You say they were not scars
but full round holes?
They used such massive nails
to hold him there?

Listen, Thomas,
I have a hammer and nails.
Not quite that size
but enough for my purpose.
And two great lengths of timber
that I could fashion
as a cross.

Let us suppose
I was dragged from my bed
and crucified
in the appointed manner.
For added irony,
let the neighbours awake
to find me hanging half-dead
in my own back garden.

Let us suppose that,
after the allotted time,
I cried out in my passion
and a passing soldier
punctured my cage
with a bayonet.

Three days later,
I was seen alive and well
by friends.

Not with friends,
mark you,
but by friends.

What would you say?

You would agree
that the whole story
was preposterous.
Of course you would.

Come on, Thomas.
You can't tell me
he somehow passed
through walls,
or still insist
that faith in this
will somehow
save my soul.

1977, 2007

View of a City Landscape

Avant garde, I'd say,
with aggressive undertones.
Possibly a comment on twentieth century
urban development.

Notice the over-use of uniformity,
the subtle suggestion of violence
through repetition.

It's generally strong on visual impact,
though some areas lack coherence.
The overall effect is disturbing, brutal,
but to be honest I rather prefer
the Constable exhibition I reviewed
last summer.

1978

Toothpaste

'Come on now, dear. You said today
you'd catch the early train.'
He stared into the bathroom sink
and cleaned his teeth, again.

'Of course my love, I'm ready now,'
he mumbled through the foam
and peered into the plughole
at the plumbing of his home.

Across the vast enamel waste
the trail of toothpaste led
into the drain's oblivion.
He wished he'd stayed in bed.

An idle thought. A protest
at the routine of his day.
If she knew half his idle thoughts,
there'd be all hell to pay.

1978

Honeysuckle

Talons in the hedgerow,
magenta red:
a ring of slender, velvet tongues.

Come close and look:
soft as a woman's lips we are,
moist with a breath of dew.

Sensuous, lascivious
unrolling of the petal:
decadent yellow ecstasy.

Limbs entwined
in passionate embrace:
wild as a gipsy lover.

1978

Prayer Of The Urban Guerilla

Moloch,
thou art mighty indeed.
There is honour in thy service:
we give thee thanks.

We measure out our praise
in sacrifice of blood.
We bless thee
for explosives and carrier bags.

Hallowed be thy name
for plate glass windows.
Thine are the shopping crowds
in busy Christmas streets.

Thine is the ageing Santa
found bleeding in his grotto.
Thine are the twisted bodies
of innocents lying dead.

We bless thee, we praise thee
for thy creation and preservation.
We give thanks to thee
for thy boundless inhumanity.

1978

Articulate Gardens

From the top of a bus
I peer into private gardens,
the much-ordered lives
of the well-to-do.

Their lawns have such a symmetry,
their flowers boast of precision:
every fibre betrays
a meticulous plan.

I am a man of simple taste
and cannot love
such articulate massacre.

Better by me
the deep reaches of the forest,
the corner of the field
untouched by the harrow's turning
where I might lie
with a lover in my arms.

1979

Jesus Saves

Give me your heart, said Jesus.
I'm a man who's used to pain.
I can straighten out your problems.
I can make you smile again.

My heart had gone to pieces.
He fixed it good and true.
Then he got me to sign this contract.
That was all I had to do.

You're alright now, he said and grinned:
the truth has found a home.
Then he hopped on a cloud to Heaven
and left me down here, alone.

1979

Incident While Walking

On the long walk
from Powerstock to Maiden Newton,
the sun slipped below
a curtain of cloud
and sent showers of golden sunset
scattering past my shoulder.

Turning to face
this intruder on my privacy,
I saw that the sun
was no taller than I
and quickly sent him packing
with a sharp cuff on the jaw.

That's enough of that, I grumbled
(all things in their appointed place)
and turned my back on summer
as the last streaks of light
melted into the deepening
autumn night.

1979

The Wrong Words

I was hoping to relieve
some private misery, redeem
the suffering, undo
the habit of pain; but my mouth
was full of razor blades, my hands
were dripping with knives.

1979

The End of the Song

This is the end of the song.
This is part the last.
There is no exposition, no development,
just this inadequate full-stop.

It is not a very convincing exit.
In fact, it is more like a beginning
than the end of action. The hero's plight
is unresolved, good and evil
still fight it out on the rooftops.

A few hours from now, the dawn patrol
will find a small body
mutilated by the years,
long impotent with doubt,
lying in a pool of unlived dreams.

1979

Surer Than the Vows

Growing older, passion subdued.
The body that had once been soft as willow
grew slack: skin stretched,
his jaw began to sag.

The supple yearning that had fired
their youthful ecstasy
the years drew to a close:
mortality grew from their limbs
like a shroud.

Reduced to such infirmity,
their lives disown affection.
The blunting habit of days
has made them sterile,
drained the lifeblood of their hopes and dreams
for this loveless, friendly tolerance.

1979

Three Dead Poems

In this briefcase,
three dead poems.
In this revolver,
three spent cartridges.

On the carpet,
a trail of blood
leads from the ghastly scene.

They died
not without screaming.
Letters of the alphabet
are spattered on the walls.
One carved a fatal message
in the plaster:
'You murdered me,
apostate!'

My suit fits most comfortably.
My neatly rolled umbrella
is standard to perfection.

My fellow travellers
appear not to have noticed
the string of wordy entrails
protruding from my luggage.

1979

Warm Flesh, Cold Bones

Behind the manicured smile,
a skeleton cloaked
in warm flesh and blood.

Poor simple creature!
In a semaphore
of wild windmill waving,
the warm flesh shouts and sings,
caresses, makes love,
breathes the invigorating air.
With each jerky movement,
the skeleton creaks more insistently.
The warm flesh breathes harder,
makes love more passionately,
strains with a new desperation
to smother the sounds
of impermanence.

Finally, the skeleton
lurches the flesh to its grave,
the rattle of cold bones
driving the beast to a frenzy.

Look at the creature run!
Feverishly clutching at life,
still unredeemed and unresolved:
forlorn and faithless harlequin
at odds with its own mortality.

1979

Trappings

A guard attends the doorway
but greets you with a smile.
You step into the sanctum
and tread the lavish pile.
You're living your ambition;
you've reached the golden mile.

You drink in your good fortune.
It's here the money's made.
It's here the future's bartered.
It's here the games are played.
You've learned the arcane jargon
and now it's time to trade.

You know you'll build a mountain
of cash up to the sky.
Whatever you should covet
you'll have the means to buy.
Then one day faithless Mammon
will hang you out to dry.

1981, 2007, 2010

Soldier

We used to shout and argue.
We used to scrap and fight.
We'd grate with every plateful
then make up overnight.

Oh how they used to tire me,
those old campaigning days.
You were a maid of passion.
I loved your winning ways.

Are all our scars now healing?
Is parting still so sweet?
My life seems pale and poorer
without that battle's heat.

1982, 2007

Suspense of the Red Envelope

Outside my door
a timber window sill,
drawing pin and
red envelope.

The red envelope contains
fifty pence.
It hangs crookedly
from the drawing pin.
A collector may call
tomorrow or the next day.

Tonight I had one pound
ninety two, but
from this wealth
fifty pence has been removed.

And until he comes, the
suspense of the red envelope
goes on.

Small change for a petty thief
or shamefully slender gift
from a man with inadequate money
to a child with inadequate limbs.

1982

The Garbage Lives

The wind today is insane.
The streets chatter with debris.
Long emptied drink tins
shudder in the gutter.
Discarded cigarette packets
limp along pavements
like hopeless, homeless strays
coveting shelter.

Every crevice is poked out:
lungfuls of dust rise up,
side-stepping, parrying
the cyclone's lunge.
I steal a glance behind me:
sapling trees point
accusing fingers;
litter swarms at my heels.

While Beaufort lashes the
howling back of the city,
cans, wrappers, fag-ends
arise and come alive.
Goodbye, sweet songbird.
Here's the aluminium shuffle.
Here's the manic flight of waste.
Here's the garbage, coming to get us.

1982, 2007

Street Poem

When the steel-plated
rubber-tyred street whale
says it is turning right
and a poor captive Jonah
peers forlornly through its massive
glass eye,
do not believe it.

You are in its way.

Every move you anticipate
is wrong.
Every position obstructs
still further
this impatient
metal-grilled
dancing partner.

Retreat to the pavement?
Seek refuge
on a traffic island?

Oh no:
you have vacillated too long,
here comes the hungry
yawning bonnet.

1982

A Small Forgotten Door

Maybe one day:
the telephone will drag me into the hall
with its customary ill-timed bleating,
and a distant heavenly voice
announce the meaning of life.

Or perhaps:
God will stumble at my door,
collapse and seek my guidance,
having lost all faith and
given up hope.

Maybe one day:
man will stop maiming man,
fear and hatred will cease,
and peace and justice
will flower upon the earth.

Or then again, perhaps
the truth will enter my heart
by a small forgotten door,
and a star will shine in a
far off galaxy.

1982, 2005

On Farley Mount

On Farley Mount
an obelisk stands tall and
yellow in the gentle
rose-petalled evening light.

Mist rises in the valley
over grey-green plumes of
tree and hedge, forms
cotton wool pools in the
meadows' hollows.

Grey feathered clouds in
a salmon-pink ceiling
garland this vision of
ancient countrymen.

We turn again to
the dry chalk path,
retrace our steps over soil
as white and dusty
as their bones.

1982

Vandalus Rusticus

I have waited for daisies
to pierce regimented lawns.
I have urged moss and clover
in the wake of motor mowers,
spawned algae in mediterranean
blue swimming pools and
strewn voracious weeds across
gravel drives and asphalt
tennis courts.

I have no constraining discipline.

I invite wild orchids to root
in the seats of luxury cars,
sturdy ivy to twine the
silver slats of radiators,
humble rust to daub its slogans
on the brilliantined coachwork

In each neurosis-tidy
manicured and sterile
artifice of rural England,
let anarchist sparrows burst into attics
at 5 a.m. daily and
riot on mutinous rafters.
Let saboteur spiders
spin savage silk webs
that snare their tormentors and
will not
be hoovered away.

1982

Carrots

Pale bleached insipid
pink fingers
factory scrubbed shrink-wrapped
and clinical
adorn the supermarket's shelves,
lie with their *rigor mortis*
like dead songbirds
in shopping trolley cages.

Hours later,
my friend calls with a
newspaper parcel.
Inside, a bunch of carrots,
fern-fronded Devon red and
damp soil caked.

1982

This is a Dangerous Place

As my dreams
give way to nightmares,
a slender grip on reality
slips away from our leaders.
I sense them growing restless
for the fallout shelter,
slavishly aching to press
the untouchable button.

I see gloomy corridors
in secret bunkers:
on flickering monitors,
cartoon cities explode
like paper bags,
whole tower blocks telescope
into shovelfuls of dust.
All insurance is vaporised
at the speed of light.

God gets the blame.
There were always zealots and bigots
slogging it out in His name.
Armageddon. The Millennium.
Now just wasted prophecies,
gone forever
in one blinding white delirious
orgasm of power ecstasy.

And then ...

System shut down.
Screens fade to black.
White noise.
Burning.
The smell of death.

1982, 2007

Craneflies

Craneflies in the kitchen.
Crazed *kamikaze* pilots
strafing the ceiling,
fatally nose-diving
the solid floor:
helter skelter madmen
with dicky motors.

I sometimes wonder
at the meanness of God.
All those craneflies with
noisy two-stroke engines
year after year setting out
on a one-way, three-day
mission.

Sopwith Camels in the age
of rockets and neutron bombs!

1982

Why November Sundays Are Loveless

That's why November Sundays are loveless,
she said.

And it was true.
Dereliction gets everywhere,
broom-bristle trees just
the thin end of the wedge.

Ridiculous bright seaside cafés,
salt-shuttered and paint-peeling,
squeak at the brooding sky.

Old lily ponds lose their magic
when the fountains shut down,
mere unadorned mirrors in the
terracotta plainness of next year's
flowerbeds.

1982

Municipal Trees

In our street, the trees
grow wild thick bristle heads
that spike the white midwinter
sky.

Their roots run deep through the
cold packed earth, under surging
mains, while their untamed hearts
turn the coil of spring's
green fuse.

Until, one day, from the
corridored bowels of the
safety-helmeted overall-clad and booted
town hall
there comes a-clanking and
a-whirring forth butchery.

STAND CLEAR!

It's the municipal chainsaw gang.

Pruning's their game and,
lining the pavements in hideous
witness to their craft,
stand long colonnades of
broken knuckles,
clenched on black-fisted stumps.

1983, 2007, 2008

A January Park Bench

Dank January day, mild and drizzling.
Puddles creeping into shoes.
Rusted gutter firing raindrops
from a corrugated roof:
tic, tac, tic, tac.

There's an empty park bench.
Its slats are grey. No one passes.
Its slats are ridged and furrowed. No one pauses.
In the leaden borders, a lone polyanthus
dazzles its setting like the lone star
in a brooding soil-and-asphalt sky.

It's different here in April.
Then, the dossers and winos come,
newsprint away whole afternoons
with old papers and carrier bags;
yesterday's stories at the
open air local social.

Grim, grey and waterlogged,
their world's deserted now;
but soon some blackened thumb
will turn the page of spring
to bring
this lost, forlorn and purposeless
January park bench to life.

1983, 2007

Ghost Train

And could it once have been that
steam trains passed this way?
Coughed, hammered, snorted through this
trail of twisted weeds?
Catapulted buck rabbit from his burrow,
scandalised timid sheep
and pounded the anvil rails
with all the sweat of miners' muscles?

Some need of that strength and power today
as we wrestle with the snagging
thorn-tangled undergrowth.
Brambles are careless of history
and scorn the navvies' labour
that laid their ballast bed.
Saplings have no memory of engineers
nor knowledge of bridges and viaducts.
Even now their deep, probing roots
suck at the very mortar that carries
their lofty, unnatural perch.

1983

Night Lines at Bursledon Station

In the inkwell river beside
rails and motorway,
the dip pen boats are bobbing:
a secretive idyll hunched behind hedges,
hiding from view of the Solent commuter.

Before the slow throbbing diesel train
nudges out of the hillside lights,
I listen.

Ignore the coarse rasp of the
petrol king. In Devon,
the home-coming cattle might once
have sounded like this.

On the ripple-combed River Hamble,
the bobbing boats slap ropes.
Masts like cowbells are ringing,
singing nocturnal soliloquy.

1984

Turl Street

Surprised in Oxford to find
Turl Street called itself,
I might have left
a hackneyed graffito
were it not for want of
white paint and a brush.

It's not that I salute
the urban vandal: rather,
with so much muck defining
England's mean, unpleasant land,
it seemed right that some street
somewhere
should be renamed
in muck's honour.

I muse on this as night revellers
stumble home past dog dung
and jettisoned takeaways,
the flagstones set like tripwires
above ground zero effluence.

This fortress of infection!
This rancid plot,
this pile, this heap,
this Turd Street!

1984, 2007, 2010

Silent Wires

The silent wires are hanging
in the still December air.
No ripples move upon the muddy pool
where wet clay clods from tractor tyres
were flung. They still lie there
dissolving, like the smoke of gathered fuel

which rises from the rooftops
of the houses on the plain
where headlamps carve a route between two towns,
the muffled shapes that pass their gaze
like ghosts. A distant train
is racing with its echo from the Downs.

My gloves are pulled on tightly
but the grip of ice grows strong.
A speckled cloak of stars will steal in soon
when knots of frost will cling to earth,
and night write winter's song
on silent wires, like staves against the moon.

1985, 2008

Culture Crash

You're getting quite accustomed
to her staring at your jokes.
She thinks it will be worth it
when at last you meet her folks.
The fearsome duty beckons
like a spanner in the spokes.

A cold and studied welcome
gives their righteousness away.
They method-act their drama
without hearing what you say.
Their mood betrays a measure
of depression and dismay.

The world's a raging furnace
for doting parents' dreams.
Life is not as imagined:
now cue the curdling screams.

Your hosts may think they suffer,
but then anguish is their style.
You're not the Boston Strangler,
but they'll doubt it for some while.
In lives of dull convention,
you're their very latest trial.

In quiet desperation,
risk subversion with a smile!

1985, 2007, 2010

As Gentle As Once She Was Proud

Time washed her life like grains of sand.
The afterglow of love once shared renewed.
The unbowed will, the reckless passion
were worn into the form of grace, and now
as gentle as once she was proud.

Her ghosts have flown like phantom clouds,
dissolving in the misty cloak of dawn.
Her days unfold like wild spring flowers
that pull the threads of winter's ashen gown.
As gentle as once she was proud.

Though she has gone, her lover's dreams
still smoulder in the embers of the fire
and where she passed, her perfume lingers:
the fragrance of the yesterdays we vowed.
As gentle as once she was proud.

1985

My Doctor's Prognosis

Remember those days at the High School?
The Aberdeen fiend in the gym?
The stale, turgid air of assembly
with orchestra slaying the hymn?
I'm still being cured of the learning.
My doctor's prognosis is grim:
'A very real danger of breakdown,
the chance of recovery slim.'

I'm riding the academe highway
with all of my erudite chums.
I'll captivate girls with my Latin,
bewitch them with fabulous sums.
We'll whisper sweet nothings from Plato.
We'll hope that the dawn never comes.
We'll muse on IQs while our young hearts
impersonate African drums.

They sold me a thinking man's future,
but then let me out of the bag.
The real world of laundry and dishes
is such an impossible drag.
The Kiplings have gone from the staff room
along with the chalk and the rag.
The sun may have set on the Empire,
but I am still waving the flag.

1985, 2002, 2009

Green Devon Hills

Stuck nose to tail
   on the Exeter bypass,
pale sunlight gleams
   on the glistening grilles.
Faint through the film
   of dead insects and car fumes,
we sometimes catch sight
   of the green Devon hills.

Green Devon hills,
   skidmarks and spills.

Stuck back to back
   in the motorway café,
limp chips in oil
   are the dish of the day.
Clocks turn to stone
   for the travel-worn masses
who gridlocked and tired
   cannot move on their way.

Move on their way,
   nowhere today.

Out on the road,
   there are sirens and rumours
and radios playing
   to spiritless crowds.
Haggard and drawn
   in the convoy of waiting,
pale faces stare out
   at the cotton wool clouds.

Cotton wool clouds,
   skidmarks and shrouds.

1985, 1998, 2010

A Cornish Lament

After Betjeman

The plume of smoke below Tresmeer has gone.
The porter and the ticket clerk have flagged the final train.
Their neatly tended flowerbeds, abandoned, run to seed.
Their station windows weep Atlantic rain.

Now lorries pound the green lanes by St. Breward
and serried ranks of cars line Padstow quay,
while buckets, spades and sun-hats storm the beaches
and surf-boards throng the angry Cornish sea.

The rugged homes that once held Bible Christians
sit cheek by jowl with bungalows that make
retirement homes for London's spent commuters,
who waste away on China tea and cake.

The plume of smoke below Tresmeer has gone.
No footsteps pace the platform edge
                        where concrete flagstones crack.
The lichen-crusted, dull and rusted paintwork floats to earth.
A kestrel eyes its prey upon the track.

1985, 1998, 2007, 2008

Minimalism

Entries in a short poem competition

I

I think I'll write a poem.
I'll make it short and sweet.
I'm sorry if I kept you.
My poem is complete.

II

Art to be smart
ought to be short.

III

Critics roar:
'Less is more!'

1985

Hard Times and Rotten Rhymes

I come home from work
and I turn on the box.
It's rhyme on the dole
from *authenticus vox*.

They're raising the flag
for the destitute north.
Muck and brass *emigrés*
boldly hold forth.

I come from the south
so I'm clearly a goon.
I open my mouth
and I rattle my spoon.

I don't understand
what it's like to be fed
on tea from a jam jar
or dripping on bread.

I measure success
by the girth of my gut
which keeps me interred
in my middle-class rut.

I come from the south
so I'm clearly a goon.
I open my mouth
and I rattle my spoon.

Contorted with comfort
and loaded with loot,
I'm clearly outmoded
and fit for the boot.

I'd publish my guilt
and confess that I'm wrong
but no one will market
a literate song.

I come from the south
so I'm clearly a goon.
I open my mouth
and I rattle my spoon.

1985

A Holiday at Home

We huddled in our shelter
as the wind whipped up the surf,
the bowling green a paddy field
of saturated turf.
The one-armed bandits clattered
in the neon-lit arcade
and space invaders plundered
as the pinball wizards played.

We paddled to the boarding house
and packed away our gloom
then paid a cheerless landlord
for the refuge of our room.
The views are not so glorious
through driving sheets of rain.
Perhaps we'll settle next year
for a package tour in Spain.

1985

Wedgwood Blues

Old Mr. Wedgwood invented a plate
to garnish the meals of the rich and the great.
Here in my hovel, it's broth from a crock
and dining on art is a cultural shock.

They've opened a showroom remote as the moon
to those not endowed with a filigree spoon.
American tourists enthuse with their wives.
No bargains at Barlaston – what a surprise!

By shelf-loads of treasure, I wearily glide
and notice the price tags are all very wide.
Across the Atlantic, these fabulous plates
will dignify burgers and chips in the States.

1985

Answer Me

Damn the modern telephone
and Alexander Bell.
The sound of his invention
has made my life a hell.

The howling of the ringtone
proclaims a new attack,
a form of sonic torture
that makes my patience crack.

Someone wants to talk to you
no matter what you'd rather do,
no matter that you've gone to bed,
no matter that you hang your head.
I will not let your senses be
until at last you answer me!

I've just sat down to dinner
or sunk into the tub.
I've found a good night's viewing
or settled for the pub.

It's then the monster summons.
Just as I reach the door,
I hear its awful anthem,
the electronic roar.

Someone wants to talk to you
no matter what you'd rather do,
no matter that you've gone to bed,
no matter that you hang your head.
I will not let your senses be
until at last you silence me!

1985, 2002, 2010

Out of Time

I've been going round in circles
since I heard the news:
lost a friend I didn't
want to lose.
You held on to your dignity
and sense of fun:
here's a small memorial from your son.

Got my family photographs:
the Grosvenor charabanc
at Brixton Green for Southend
and the sea.
There's a toddler in a sun-hat
with a plastic spade at Greatstone,
wide-eyed as the sand dunes:
that was me.

Perhaps in time
a boy of mine
will live to hear the stories
that go with these old emblems
of the past.
I never thought your time
would run so fast.

I've been going round in circles
since I heard the news:
lost a friend I didn't
want to lose.
You held on to your dignity
and sense of fun:
here's a small memorial from your son.

Please take this small memorial
from your son.

1985

The Racer

My friends are getting stout and fat
but I shall never be like that.
With saddle, spoke and alloy rim
I fight the flab and keep in trim.

I ride the road with iron nerve
where motor dodgems snarl and swerve.
Not for me a box of tin.
I turn pedals, I stay thin.

1986

On Spetisbury Station, Dorset

For Denis Baxter

The pub remains, where fading prints
    recall the age of steam,
but no one climbs the platform steps,
    now cloaked in rampant green;
and through these hills, that fire and steel
    will never sound again.
'There'll be no more a-rushin'
    to catch the Spetisbury train.'

1986

Fishbourne Signal Box, Sussex

The signal box by Fishbourne Road
   still stands?
I thought that cost accountancy
   had swept such things away.
Then bells still sound the trains
   to Portsmouth Harbour?
And polished levers set the road,
and log-book entries measure out
   each day?

The signal box by Fishbourne Road
   still stands:
a modern rail anomaly
   where section codes still chime.
Old rods and gates hold on
   in this backwater,
where semaphores, tied cottages,
and cables, locks and pulleys work
   out time.

1986, 2007

Tarmac

The oilfields are burning,
the world's in a mess,
so get on the motorway!
Drive to excess!
The rev counter's rising,
it's tarmac on earth.
May all who oppose us
be strangled at birth.

The ozone's dissolving?
The poles come apart?
We still have our freedom,
so drivers take heart!
With temperatures climbing,
there's fun on the beach
(as long as a boom keeps
the oil out of reach).

So on with our engines!
Let's rev and be green!
Those clever converters
make motoring clean.
Oh, carbon dioxide?
As harmless as lead.
The trees give off that, or
so some scientist said.

1991

Art

I

I write a thousand lines a day
but no one reads a word I say,
and all this labour on my part
produces not one jot of art.

A wizard at the silver screen,
I conjure spells in black and green,
but though my magic may be smart
the masses know it is not art.

The all-consuming chip and pad
devoured the life I might have had,
but restless still, my hollow heart
in search of purpose yearns for art.

II

My peace of mind was dearly bought;
this stuff is harder than I thought.
It rots my brain, and doctors chart
the pain that I endure for art.

III

I opened up my threadbare soul
and hoped that words would make it whole
but, though I played the poet's part,
they left me wanting more than art.

I fumbled at the chapel door
and lightly trod its hallowed floor,
but though the music tugged my heart
I knew that it was only art.

My holy grail was all along
some sweet seductive siren song,
but wiser now, I'll shortly start
to seek a substitute for art.

IV

Still waiting by the chapel door,
no wiser than he was before,
he trod the boards and played his part
convinced that there was life in art.

1997, 1999

Winter

I was waiting for the warning call of winter.
There were bare trees in the garden
and the heating on inside,
when the dawn threw on its jacket with a shiver
and the crunch of frosted leaves
betrayed my footfalls on the drive.

There were choristers and anthems in the chapel.
There were icicles like organ pipes
that glistened in the eaves.
There were dappled dancing shadows, and a sundial
on a glinting granite plinth
among the marble-headstoned graves.

I was sacred for a moment on that morning,
but I thought of my near future
as the ground pressed to my feet.
There was hemlock in the sting of winter's stirring,
and the shrivelled shoots of autumn
laid like embers in the grate.

1997, 1998

Till Easter Dawns Again

The white surf spins a mist of salty spray.
A passing sea-wife tugs her billowed hood.
The season's done. The crowds have sailed away
and ice cream parlours closed their doors for good.

The harbour bandstand waits in stately pose,
its chapel hymns and village silver gone,
while gingham-patterned tearoom tables doze
behind mock-Georgian windows on the prom.

Along the fish-damp streets, the muffled light
from sailors' bars exudes a faded charm.
Then rain comes, pulsing stardust in the night,
and couples scurry homeward, arm in arm,
to bolted doors, drawn curtains and log fires.
Till Easter dawns again, the town retires.

1997

Sight

Once in a life, perhaps, some gentle soul
will meet our eyes and gaze into our heart,
and see there not so much the years' long toll
as all the love that we might yet impart.

Once in a life, perhaps, this stranger's care
will stir in our lost longings some recall
of every moment we had yearned to share
and make us wish that we could give them all.

I know at last how I became aware
of your sweet grace in my poor lifeless days,
though now the mocking of your empty chair
confounds my sight and muddles all my ways.

Once in my life, I glimpsed what might have been
and opened my eyes to see as I was seen.

1998, 2005, 2010

Identity Crisis

I don't want to be a poet.
Neat stanzas are not for me.
I wish that my view of the cosmos
derived from a colour TV.

I don't want to write in couplets.
I don't want to think in verse.
They're rhyming my mind to distraction.
My muse is a perfect curse.

I long for the languid lifestyle:
some billiards down at the club,
a feast from some Indian menu,
a liquid dessert in the pub.

There'll be no distress in the morning,
no anguish or doubt at man's fall.
The spiritual world will elude me.
The hangover cure will be all.

I'll focus my mind on the present,
let God-fearing faith all dissolve.
A lottery win in an instant
will serve as my only resolve.

I don't want to be a poet.
Oh, why can't my soul agree
when matters of metaphysics
are mystery all to me?

1998

Flame

I came upon your picture. Like a ghost
it haunted me. Adrift, my mind unwound
the tangled web of years that must have passed
between our last farewell and where I stand.

I fell upon your memory. Like a flame
it fired me, warm and close as we had been.
Through earth's cold separation, you had come
in mystery and love to stem my pain.

1998

Had and Held

It was the end of things. All trust was lost,
all care had gone and passion turned to sand.
The sterile nights accrued the mounting cost
of words unsaid. A numbness gripped her hand.

It was the death of things. Their lives turned strange,
the days a snare of drudgery and chores.
Only their spirits pleading for some change
sustained the hope that life might yet be more.

Habit consumed all things and, pleasure past,
they mimed a daily litany of need,
as though in silence they might find at last
some nourishment on which their souls might feed.

The doorbell rings to find them both at home
but, in their hearts, the loveless live alone.

1998

Cleeve Abbey

The walls of hand-hewn stone where plaster fell
gave up the secrets of their masons' care
some centuries ago. The office bell
that measured out the daily round of prayer

has fallen too, and now the camera's whir
enunciates this relic's modern rite,
the vision of its saints a myth-like blur
of something half-perceived in fading light.

It was not always so. The country wife
who worked the farmhouse range believed in God
and, in familiar faith, did not view life
as His poor finite gift, nor thought it odd
to see the cattle cross the cloister garth
from mullioned arcade windows by the hearth.

1998

Sunday Morning With Tricycle

A sombre pair drive past in stately splendour
and hearse-like reverence. Off to church,
　　　no doubt.
I turn the pedals, gain the road and over
humps and potholes slowly lurch
　　　about.

My three-wheeled progress keeps the kids contented
but speed is relative. When they cry
　　　'Faster!',
I press down harder. Though all our weight combined
prohibits haste, the car is not my
　　　master.

1998

The Invisible Man

The invisible man at the doorway
slips in as the bolt is shot.
The children see him, but they believe
in miracles, fairies, Christmas ...
    Their mother does not.

They've seen him at work in the garden
or cursing at things gone wrong.
When toys are broken, they raise his name
with sellotape, cardboard, scissors ...
    The magic is strong.

The invisible man at the doorway
takes shape in the shadowed hall.
He sees the children, and wonders how
their miracle came to happen ...
    None answers his call.

1998, 2005

Wight: Deep Low, Falling

Atlantic storms come in like
Viking raiders: hungry, cruel,
virile, wild from days of spray
and cold salt rations. Landfall
is their prey.

The suburbs shudder, sensing
plunder's path. The pots on ageing
chimneys chatter. Carrier bags balloon
like longship sails and rocket skywards,
life-aspiring,

freed at last from gravity's thrall.
Limp fences grimace, creak and groan
as larch succumbs to splinters. The ricochet
brings faces to grey windows, weeping rain.
Meanwhile, a roof tile slithers.

Umbrella spokes lie strewn on
emptied pavements, like fishbones
where some ogre gorged. The
useless, pristine handle gauntly grips
a black skin flap.

The sky is breathing umber like a
cauldron from the sea. The streets
are lashed and savaged.
Sheets of sodden flotsam slide
beneath my feet.

I stagger on more urgently, my
mind adrift, rehearsing useless strategies.
What sanctuary could lurk in these
dank passageways, where shapes and shadows
fuse in phantom grey?

Talons of salt spray finger my coat-tails.
Oaths and curses whirl in the wind. Now
I claw each step from the ground, but
it slips beneath me: brazen Saxon,
fallen knave.

1999, 2002, 2010

Stogumber Station

A station here? No, who would think
that village folk would traipse the lanes,
or tramp the hedgerow-bordered fields
to catch infrequent broad gauge trains?

But come they did. All third class fares,
no doubt, from coomb and hillside farms,
whose busy, bustled wives would wait
with wicker baskets crook'd in arms.

A small red sandstone lodge provides
the booking hall. The rest is made
of wood, and occupies a ledge
carved from a scarp with pick and spade.

The goods shed and the camping coach
are gone, yet lanterns have returned
to light the platform after dark,
though no more paraffin is burned,

but eco bulbs. Still, that's no price
for gleaming steam trains to the coast
some forty years since men in suits
decreed that profit matters most.

I sit here dreaming. Blackbirds sing
sweet phrases from a timeless tune,
while water-spangled ferns collect
the haze of August afternoon.

2001

Powerstock

Memories of West Dorset, 1975

Say, do branch trains pause at Powerstock still
on the lonely line under Eggardon Hill?
No, there are foxes and brambles there,
and the railway's course is bereft and bare.
But the lanes remain silent, then as now,
bar the wheeling gulls and the lumbering plough.

Say, are there crimson cider apples still
in the tumbling orchard by the gnarled old mill?
No, there are nettles and rosebay there,
hiding clay tiles cracked by the sky's long glare.
But the stone-flecked stream turns its warp of weeds
while the waving grasses hang their heads with seeds.

There were silver shafts of dust-speckled light
as the sun declined into late summer night,
years in the scrubbed wooden table's grain
mapped in shadows cast from a cobwebbed pane.
The door opened out to a stone-clad street,
then the station hill, and the whispering wheat.

2002, 2005

The Winchester Diver

He 'saved the cathedral with his own two hands' –
King George V, 1912

The great alone do not possess this place,
though tableaux, tombs and chantries might suggest
that benefactors viewed eternal rest
as more the gift of wealth than holy grace.

The sons of nameless clay may have no face
preserved in sculptured stone, yet they possessed
the will to save the Cromwell-shattered west
front glass, when arms would raze it without trace.

They matter still. A diver made his name
by stealing the cathedral from a grave
of water, peat and bone. In liquid earth
for sightless years he toiled, and though his fame
felt undeserved, his hands had helped to save
a treasured house. His work revealed his worth.

2002

The Ministry of Time

My limbs are growing frail and weak,
and joints, once supple, ache and creak.
My laughing, fearless daughters tease
that I am heir to ills like these.

My thatch has thinned. The mighty comb
has called my crown of plenty home.
And, as my girls demurely say,
what still remains is turning grey.

My smile betrays a buckled bite
where wisdom teeth and molars fight,
and orthodontic surgeons muse
on which incision they would choose.

My face is furrowed, lines and cracks
my due in lost youth beauty tax,
the only thing that blossoms there
the wire wool of my facial hair.

The shaving mirror on the wall
reflects my slow decline and fall.
To all we are, our breath, our name,
the ministry of time lays claim.

2002

Lost

The pearls of frost are melting on the lawn
where once we stood. A cloak of silk betrays
the pale, half-shrouded sun, whose rising dawn
invokes the ghost of poignant, parting days.

Its utter silence makes the moment strange:
no bird sings, and the buds are far from birth;
a secret world, an instant without change
where past and present share the haunted earth.

I thought I saw you walking through the grass,
that half-smile on your lips, and eyes that fixed
on mine, though reason said you could not pass
this way again. I ache with sorrow, mixed
with that sweet tenderness you gave to me;
still lost in all that I no longer see.

2002

Clouds

Gazing through the glazing in the ceiling,
the lazy tufts of cumulus float by.
Their blushing luminescence signals evening
beyond my narrow vision of the sky.

The subject, it would seem, is motivation,
and how to make reluctant learners learn.
I wonder, do those windows really open?
What subterfuge of hinges makes them turn?

Gazing through the glazing in the ceiling,
the wisdom of the lecturer drifts by.
The whited walls reverberate with learning,
but I would rather sit beneath the sky.

2003

Little Things

It's the little things that matter,
like the unexpected chatter
of a friend whom we did not expect to meet.
These simple things can make our life seem sweet.

It's the bigger things that rattle,
that will shake off every chattel
on a day when there's another world to greet.
What final hand will make our life complete?

2003

The Voice

Our voices deafen
the least heard, the quiet voice
trapped inside our head.

2003

The Train Cometh Not

New words for 'The Gas Man Cometh'
by Michael Flanders and Donald Swann

'Twas on a Monday morning
    I was shaken out of bed
by the roar of an alarm clock
    which exploded in my head.
I staggered to the station
    but discovered with a cuss
that the engineers weren't finished,
    so we'd have to catch a bus.
Oh, it's endless fun
    on a long commuting run.

'Twas at the nearby junction
    that they waved away the train
before we could get on it,
    so we waited in the rain.
At last, another rumbled in
    just twenty minutes late;
four grime-encrusted carriages
    which normally are eight.
Oh, it's endless fun
    on a long commuting run.

'Twas only one stop further
    that we halted yet again;
our driver had been rostered
    on the next returning train.
We waited at the platform
    while they struggled on the 'phone
to find another crewman who
    was spare, and still at home.
Oh, it's endless fun
    on a long commuting run.

At last, a cab delivered him
    and we were off to work.
(Employers are inclined to think
    that all we do is shirk.)

We'd covered fifteen miles before
    the next announcement said
our train was now so late
    that it would terminate instead.
Oh, it's endless fun
    on a long commuting run.

'Twas at another junction
    we were all put out once more,
but the carriage lock jammed open
    and I couldn't shut the door.
A fitter came to fix it
    but he shook his head and said
the whole thing was unsafe
    and should be moved into the shed.
Oh, it's endless fun
    on a long commuting run.

By now the sun was setting
    so I knew the time had come
when I should turn around and
    undertake the homeward run.
I left the heaving booking hall
    to find the nearest bank,
withdrew a fist of notes
    and hailed a taxi at the rank.
Oh, it's endless fun
    on a long commuting run.

I wondered as the wind picked up
    and leaves began to fall
whether it might not be better
    if they ran no trains at all.

Life is not much fun
    till commuting days are done.

2003

Silent Night

No cars, no dogs, no parties,
no roaring drunk in song,
no flattened drink-can football,
but stillness all night long.

No neon haze, no floodlights,
no screaming jet-pierced sky,
but wide-eyed crystal darkness
to watch the stars go by.

No cat-claw screech and wailing,
no couple turned to hate,
no siren flashing fury,
no flailing broken gate.

No motorway, no lorries,
no gridlocked rat run queue,
no diesel-blackened curtains,
but mist and morning dew.

2003

Fizzy Feet

I'm known as 'Little Widdle',
or else as Heather Jane.
I'm not exactly normal.
It's tricky to explain.

My dad is tall and noisy.
My mum is short and sweet.
My sister's got teenitis,
but I've got fizzy feet.

They fizzle when it's bedtime.
They fizzle through the night.
They sizzle in the bedclothes
until the morning light.

Can't weigh them down with concrete.
Can't stick them down with glue.
My feet are just so fizzy!
Whatever can I do?

2003

Hands

Hands that are gentle
hands that caress
hands that know sorrow
wrung in distress

Hands that know anger
hands that know pain
hands that have laboured
long without gain

Hands that are wrinkled
hands that are old
hands that are lonely
gnarled by the cold

Hands with arthritis
hands without form
hands without vigour
twisted and torn

Your hands
My hands

2003

Shopping for Culture

It used to be a bookshop.
Once.

Hardy, Dickens, Priestley
graced the shelves,
and sometimes a few
of the safer names
in modern verse:
Auden, Betjeman, or that
Liverpool wordsmith who
wanted to die
a young man's death.

Fat chance of culture now!

The sixties' soccer genius
working through his second liver
vies with the fresh-faced undergrad
who won a TV talent show.

Superficially,
the choice is vast:
sport and celebrities,
washed up politicians,
next year's travel guides
(already obsolescent),
ghost writers, utter nonentities
and those who might be
voices from the grave ...
all raking the embers
of fleeting, failing fame.

Remaindered stock turns up in a store
at the meaner end of town,
but starts life here:
glossy tomes of vacuous prose
doomed for the groaning
coffee table, which creaks beneath
its load of leaden words.

English Lit hangs on in a rack
of glossy, thin revision guides
devoured by schoolkids
cramming Shakespeare,
the towering genius on these shelves
an author whose book's worth opening
more than once.
(A dictionary, perhaps?)

I scan the racks in vain
for the latest, shocking *exposé:*
Decline and Fall of the English Bookshop,
a study in tabloid tyranny.

2003

Fifty Years On

Fifty years on from a boy in the sand
and my eyes wide with innocent fun,
a photo-survivor from old make-and-mend
when the world wore a smile and the sun always shone.

Fifty years on from a brick terraced house,
though the street was a phoenix in flame;
now high-rise grotesque like a gross Trojan horse,
giving ancient mad planners the lie to a dream.

Fifty years on from the great post-war boom
and my dreaming has gone down the drain.
This pile of debris was once *crème de la crème*
and the coins in my pocket once knew how to shine.

But fifty years on, or a hundred years on,
who will remember when my cares are gone?

2004

Christmas Pays

'Christmas comes but once a year – small mercy.'
'Don't ask me now, there's so much left to do.'
Children in a frenzy, parents shirty.
 'I can't stand crowds and, God, the endless queues!'

'I'll put it on the credit card.' 'And how
will *that* be paid?' 'We'll find a way, *okay?*'
'You know I'm busy. Please, just leave it out.'
'I've had enough. I'm calling it a day.'

The mission bell's forgotten. Christmas pays.
The high street stores praise Jesus on their tills
and, bagging up the money, count each day's
reward. Half the world starves. The rest seems ill.

Somewhere, a helpless child lies in a stall.
God, was it meant to be like this at all?

2004

The Cause of my Disillusion

The cause of my disillusion
I traced to a faulty brain.
The need for its total re-wiring
was manifest, urgent and sane.

I went to the doctor, who asked me,
'Are you sure you want this done?
I've never tried this procedure.
It could all go horribly wrong.'

I settled the fee, then in theatre
bowed down to the surgeon's knife.
I knew that the risk I was taking
was bound to improve my life.

So many things now seem uncertain
of which I was then so sure.
I'll never pretend to myself again
that a transplant could be my cure.

2004, 2010

Post Modern Batpoem

After Adrian Henri

Take me back to 1960
    Batman
DC Comics, Gotham City
    Batman
Richard Green as Robin Hood
TV puppets made from wood
All our heroes clean and good
    Batman

Modern life is unforgiving
    Batman
Take me back to easy living
    Batman
Rolls of caps, a Lone Star gun
Paddling pools and summer sun
String and conkers, one on one
    Batman

Now the world is electronic
    Batman
I can't cope, I feel moronic
    Batman
Nothing works quite well enough
Bought the upgrade but it's duff
Pen and paper, that's the stuff
    Batman

Take me back to 1960
    Batman
When the style was not so glitzy
    Batman
Shine that Batsign in the night
Save me from my deadly plight
Out of touch and out of sight
    Batman

2004

Black and White

A morning meditation

Arabica filters through the cone
into an ageing smoked-glass mug,
vestige and token of days long past.
I hold it to the light
against the bare trees in the garden.
There's a view. It's faint, distorted, tall,
'through a glass darkly' – like St. Paul,
at sea in the pagan night.

Priests name it a gift – that faith
to glimpse through doubt and disbelief
some hint of the divine.
I take my coffee white
and pour in a slug of pasteurised:
swirling, curling, bending, blending,
gone all transparency – here's the opaque;
gone all metaphors – here's the finite.

2004, 2010

Eat What You Kill

It was always competition with you,
the driven need to outperform the rest.
'Success through knowledge' –
                    how that knowledge grew!
The cash pile and the mansion prove who's best.

The mobile phone's the engine of the real
that keeps the cogs all churning, screw on screw.
Punch the numbers, nail the client, cook the deal.
Eat what you kill – there's money in the stew.

But could your one-way love become a curse?
Spell out your secrets in a crowded room?
She never cared for you and, what is worse,
may hunger for a younger suitor soon.

She has no sense of loyalty. Her flight
is certain, and your grip on life is slight.

2005

Travelling Blind

We labour long and hope it is not vain
to think that we might yet possess a dream;
but this and every day, a stale refrain
invades the hours – a joyless, dull routine.

We are the muted crowd on bus or train.
We gaze upon each season's changing scene,
yet hardly seem to notice all the pain
inside the paper; but there the words can't scream.

There's nothing left to move us any more.
Inured and listless, still we carry on,
but rarely stop to question what it's for
or wonder where the missing ones have gone.

We live by rote – a mass unconscious mind
of still-born souls; a nation of the blind.

2005, 2008, 2009

Ghosts on the Beach

Blue Anchor Bay, Somerset

The road's almost straight
    as it swaggers down the hill,
past the white crossing gates
    that snare the traffic still,
to a flat-pebbled shore
    and a boy with a kite
waging string-tangled war
    with its promises of flight.

There's a full moon tonight
    and a ship in the bay
when the sands will gleam bright
    and the wise look away,
for there's no honest trade
    needs the cloak of the dark
or polite masquerade
    from the parson and the clerk.

In their crinoline skirts
    and their stiff Sunday best
worn at chapel or church
    on their one day of rest,
all the girls from the farms
    and the men from the mines
eye the camera's charms
    and are petrified in time.

The road's almost straight
    as it swaggers down the hill,
past the white crossing gates
    that snare the traffic still,
to a desolate beach
    and a wide, yawning sky
and a past out of reach
    like the nimbus scudding by.

2005

Ode to a Barbecue

I heard a party in a nearby house.
Incipient rumblings told of wholesale booze
that, late at night, would vent in raucous shouts
from guests who'd managed to drown their IQs.

I smelt a singeing from a nearby fire.
The petro-chemicals mingled with the fumes
from something's sacrificial funeral pyre.
Was it food? Smoke cast a withering gloom

over fences to houses down the road.
Good God – it's 2 a.m., and still the noise
roars on. Not burned out yet; – the sleep I'm owed.
Bring superbrew to stupefy the boys!

The girls are already half comatose
as I plot the range of the garden hose ...

2005

I'll Never Be Romantic

I'll never be a Byron,
a Shelley or a Keats.
No high class babes are waiting
to meet me in the sheets.

I haven't got an abbey
to shoot up when I'm tight.
My friends just won't get legless,
or trash the place, or fight.

I haven't got a fortune
to dissipate in Rome.
The grandest tour I manage
is of pubs around my home.

I've not got stoned on opium
or lived at life's extremes.
The gambling debts I boast of
are a figment of my dreams.

I've never fought a duel
in a dew-soaked morning glade.
I've not been stopped by lead shot
or the rapier's deadly blade.

I'm ten miles from romantic,
some suburb's unknown son.
I'll never make the big time
with all I haven't done.

2005

Prayer

London, 7th July 2005

If prayer is the means of talking to God,
what need do the faithful have for a bomb?
Has he gone a bit deaf? Or has he trod
the paths of peace too long? Why, why a bomb?

Is the cry for a *jihad* now so loud
that the faith it corrupts needs a bomb?
What worm wishes death on an innocent crowd?
What hatred is holy? Why, why a bomb?

Westerners mired in material wealth
may not be fit for God's judgement. Let God
be their judge, not some secret assassin.

No creed can lay claim to full spiritual health.
Let hate own its name, and its death wish and blood,
and its lies and its bomb, and oblivion.

2005, 2006

Another Life

The nights draw in and darkness brings its clamour
of old regrets and sorrows left to lose,
but I would be your knight in shining armour
if I could have another life to choose.

A moment touching tenderness lies waiting,
a moment unencumbered by the past.
I'd be your guardian angel through all grieving
if I could know the choices that would last.

We spend our lives in faithful separation,
adrift, off course and many miles from shore;
survivors on the all-consuming ocean
with signals sending unread semaphore.

The nights draw in and darkness brings its clamour
of old regrets and sorrows left to lose,
but am I left, weighed down by rusted ardour,
with bridges burned and nothing left to choose?

2005, 2008, 2010

A Man of England

I am a man of England
but cultured I am not
and when I've had some Special
I really lose the plot.

I run a big old motor
but drive like Mr. Toad
and treat the slow and feeble
like vermin in the road.

Chuck it out the window.
Feel the mighty beat.
Sock it to the neighbours
half way down the street.

I buy *The Daily Knocker*
to keep up with the news
and shout down any know-all
who contradicts my views.

The ones who really nark me
fall over with a thud.
(I blame my education –
they branded me a dud.)

Raise the flag for England!
Let the people roar!
All the world's a playground
red in tooth and claw.

I wonder whose graffiti
appeared outside last night
or which dumb son of sorrow
got knocked up in a fight?

A trail of blood and vomit
now punctuates the yard.
I am a man of England.
This is my calling card.

2005

At the School of Monetary Art

Today we will study the works
of great accountants.
Dollar, Sterling and Euro
will be our guides.

Students taking the black economy option
should meet in the darkened alleyway
running surreptitiously behind this building.
(Please excuse the smell of the drains.)

The poor can obtain microscopes
from the porter, and are recommended to sit
hunchbacked
searching for their earnings potential.

All trade must be recorded except that done in
cash, which frequently causes amnesia.
What cannot be taken as cash
should be claimed as expenses.

The two minute silence for the owners
of now worthless investments has been
cancelled
due to lack of sympathy.

At lunchtime, there will be a feast
to celebrate Mammon, who recently
sold his family's business for 91 million
and laid off all the staff.

Suspicions of a social conscience
proved unfounded, but the family members
Parsimony, Greed and Hypocrisy
are helping police with their enquiries.

God is not relied on,
nor expected to announce
a final dividend
at close of business.

2005

The Week

This was a week that deafened:
all seamless days of howling,
roaring noise – no sanctuary
in its hours, the minutes scowling.

This was a week that fought back:
my clumsy bones mount the staircase,
seeking sleep – its memory follows, screams
from the bathroom mirror into my face.

This is the week that is dying,
and with it some peace in me,
neglected tasks conspiring, waiting
to snare me in any week's lee.

2006

Three Seasons

The light had failed, and shadows shunned
a world betrayed by the fleeting sun.
I stumbled through the blinding gloom
to a future dark as a waiting tomb.

Then ice came hard, like a dagger drawn
from a black night's sheath in a frozen dawn.
The savage wind had a touch like stone
and a blade that sliced through flesh to bone.

Even now, as spring cuts through the shroud
and the green shoots billow, heads unbowed,
pure steel pervades the enfolding sky
and the bare trees murmur, 'Born to die'.

2006, 2010

Mirror, Mirror

The mirror returns me a dubious look:
a life on this planet brings beauty to book,
but the health farm won't get me. The mad are okay
with a future that's measured in crumpled decay.

I rant at the TV – the outlook is slim.
It's manicure, pedicure, massage and gym.
Prized glamour pursues all the pennies we earn
for a glossy self-image in which we will burn.

And fleshy enticements warn: 'Uniform grey
is the tone of the future!' Unless we all pay,
the undercoat genes will erupt from our skin,
which grows ever wrinkled, and sallow, and thin.

I'll give back that mirror my withering look.
The reaper's grim scythe has my bones on the hook,
but I'll not yearn for youth, or submit to its rule.
Be old and defiant, not Vanity's fool!

2006

In a Sussex Lane

Riding by, I glimpsed two poppies,
high in the bank where the hedgerow parted,
bowed in prayer over tangled roots
where the furtive dunnock darted.

Of course, I'd seen poppies before,
though not this singular, shocking splash
recalling Flanders fields in a Sussex lane:
the azure sky, stained by a crimson gash.

2006

Your Special Day

I'm searching in the card shop.
Each awful, sickly line
coats sentimental drivel
in lush, romantic slime.

'I'll love you till forever
and always you'll be mine.'
The versifier's mangle
wrings out another rhyme.

Oh gushing love eternal!
Oh groaning, vapid verse!
Oh nauseous reaction!
What poem could be worse?

2006

A Somerset Reverie

I love to laze in the evening sun
with the cattle lowing and the last train gone,
as the ebbing flames of the smouldering sky
light the wrinkled sand of the wave-lapped bay.

I love to walk on the tall ridged hills
with the salt wind blowing from the sea-backed fields,
as the trail descends into witching woods
hiding live green stones in their layered shades.

I love to dream in an oak-beamed bar
with the log stumps glowing in an iron-red fire,
as the world runs wild on its half-crazed course
and the idle wise drain the warming glass.

Must all be flotsam on a mad wave's roar?
I wish, I wish that these hours were more.

2006

Mapping the Past

Close on two millennia since the Romans came,
the modern Sussex map still bears their imprint
in small, half-noticed details – the road turning
suddenly straight, or long departed features
recalled in gothic font: the rural villa,
the signal post with a view to plain and sea.

Concealed below the soil remains a layer
where Roman steps fell hard on the Downland clay,
and Celtic ways were pressed to a foreign mould,
shaping something new: a modern world, vanished
beneath the sod, its lives and loves and rhythms
reduced to muted signs on a printed page.

2006

DIY

The kitchen is swimming in six-packs and kegs.
We've gobbled the goodies and drained all the dregs.
My fair weather friends say they've done with me all
and drunkenly kicked down the door in the hall.

A blast of cold air crashes in from the street
to challenge my stupefied fingers and feet.
Here comes the brimstone, then ashes and sack.
The meter hits zero and turns my world black.

I slide into morning with hammer in head,
a mouth dry as plaster and legs full of lead.
The DJ's brash barrage increases the pain
as radio power chords drill through my brain.

2006

Advent Sneaks In

Advent sneaks in with the season of mists
while we are hurriedly still making plans,
cashing in savings and drawing up lists,
busy to burst with no time on our hands.

Advent sneaks in like a thief at the door,
stealing our moments and cramming our lives.
Christmas cards, shopping days, what's it all for?
Polish the silver and sharpen the knives!

Advent sneaks in when the year's nearly done,
fresh with expenses and tidings of toil,
fields without colour and days without sun,
time ever winding its tightening coil.

True Advent should herald a time of new birth,
a time to end waiting for God's reign on earth;
a child to redeem us by love's healing power,
a time that is God's time – and this is His hour.

2006

Credo

I am not an optimist. I am cynical,
and blame my disillusion. What
I was taught to strive and yearn for
seems now such improbable rot.

I learned to value different things;
things with no value, apparently.
I can find comfort in that, but still
rage at vain wealth, incessantly.

2006

Getting in the Stride

My father's piano

There was always a piano in the house,
slightly neglected, but still dusted or
polished weekly – a sort of bedridden
old relative: immobile, vast and stately.
Family photos stood arrayed on the lid:
black and white portraits of baby siblings,
barely at an age to sit still long enough
for the shutter's closing on some stylised scene.

It could have been a whale, beached in the lounge
we knew as the 'front room': a special place for guests
and Christmas, and the tray of drinks which maybe
had some hand in my father's animation
on such festive days as these. Unannounced,
the music started, and the silent, useless
mahogany would sing, transformed at last
to a thing of beauty, ringing out its purpose.

You would not expect a wartime family
blitzed in blazing London to favour solemn
classics: it was Fats Waller, Hoagy Carmichael
and Nat King Cole for us. He could sing too,
no mean surprise for an eldest son, like his
swaggering bass lines which could have come
from some huge black jazzman in America's south.
And I never told him once how good he was.

2007

The Fall and Rise of St. George

For the patronal festival at St. George's Church, Whyke

I go to a church called St. George's.
Our patron's a popular saint,
but thanks to the work of Pope Leo
his halo, at times, has been faint.

Apocryphal saints were demoted
for want of historical clout;
then Calendars showed them as 'options'
for none but the local devout.

The battle cry written by Shakespeare
named Harry and England and George;
for Leo, the stuff of mere legend,
a myth that Crusaders had forged.

So George was condemned to a half-life,
a spectre with only a name;
a meaningless church dedication,
a ghost unentitled to fame.

Of course, there were countries that kept him
as national saint, just like ours;
but then devolution's arrival
restored all his weakening powers.

At once, George was symbol of England
and suddenly king of the road;
no more some discarded old fashion,
but iconic national code.

So where are we now in his story?
St. George has returned to the fold.
Again, the Church Calendar names him
a true patron saint, as of old.

Pope Leo propelled him to purdah,
but just who holds whom in his thrall?
Or is there a scent of suspicion
that popular will conquers all?

2007

Mantra

Sign the contract, stay alive.
Battle through the nine-till-five.
Mind and body ache with toil.
Who will cheat the hungry soil?

Check the payslip, count the cash.
Gamble on the mortal stash.
Labour, profit, spend, invest.
Who will buy eternal rest?

Take the poisoned chalice, then;
hand it to the sons of men.
Drink it down and slake your thirst.
Who will think of worlds reversed?

2007

Night and Day

I thought I had some time to kill,
but now the doctor says I'm ill
and must submit to his regime
or float away on Dante's stream.

Devouring tablets night and day,
I keep the deadly stroke at bay
and cheat the cardiac arrest
which waits to grip me by the chest.

I cannot hope for respite now,
for life has caught me. This is how
I'll learn to name the chemist friend
and borrow time until my end.

2007

Deluge

Summer in Sussex, 2007

Gazing through the window at the seamless grey
of sky and sloping slate, the deluge spews
on to my flat felt roof. Loose chippings skate
into the gutter, while running water slews
across the pane. *'Precipitation (noun):*
fall of rain' hardly does this justice.
From some Atlantic cauldron, monstrous clouds
lash hail on summer with utmost prejudice.

A hundred miles away, a friend is washed out
from his home, the flood too fast for sandbags.
We are the lucky ones, all wide-eyed at
the glass but silently wondering what dregs
of pleasure await us: what winsome breezes;
what carefree ways before summer ceases.

2007

Hedgehog Duty

Tonight, I saw a hedgehog
but the creature spotted me
too soon to reach the safety of the verge.
He stopped at once: but freezing
at the junction of these streets
is not a wise or life-preserving urge.

I knew he had no concept
of the cruel pneumatic tyre,
his instinct honed to raise his spines, and wait.
That may deter the cat, but
here in town, machines conspire
to speed defensive hedgehogs to their fate.

I stepped into the road and,
with my foot, applied a nudge.
I heard his claws go lightly into skid.
I tried again, but clearly
he was programmed not to budge,
and heedless of the safety if he did.

The looming cars' dipped headlamps
filled the street with steely light,
illumining the drama as they passed:
my turn of hedgehog duty
at the junction in the night,
a dangerous and erinaceous task.

At last, the street turned silent
so I slipped behind a hedge
and, when I dared to look, my charge had gone
back to the world of hedgehogs:
no more living on the edge,
no tyres, no metalled road to crush him on.

The world escaped to normal
and its dull suburban sounds,
the passing cars a mortal threat no more.
Perhaps on mellow evenings
when the hedgehogs do their rounds,
I'll see him padding safely on the lawn.

2007

Light Pollution

It's never quite dark with this light pollution,
but yes: it helps when the batteries give out
and I'm forced to follow the road by cloud,
up-lit by the sprawl. Shine on, sodium!

That sprawl sits low on the plain's horizon,
unseen by day; but at night it's revealed
by its nebula, the darkness dissolved
in a strange skyscape of man-made photons.

With that, the real sky goes to oblivion,
yet the single point of riding these lanes
was to see it, and sample solitude.

There's the rub. The world is always turned on,
and this nimbus cover makes it a bane:
all around me, the teeming multitude.

2007

Before the Fall

We posture like gods.
Below us, the breakers roar
like crashing fortunes.

2007, 2008

Radio Days

It was all much slower then, with the valves
taking time to warm to their daily task.
To a toddler, the voices were magical,
conjured to life through a cloth-grilled mask.

What were the programmes then?
                              Light, Home and Third,
laced with faraway place names on the dial:
Hilversum, Athlone, Moscow, Luxembourg;
a chant heavy-laden with post-war style.

Fast forward fifty years, and what have we got?
We rode technology's super-highway
but missed the sign for sophistication.

The moving image rules the waves, but not
this heart. Budget TV begets decay.
Entertainment becomes aberration.

2008

Generations

After school, it was always the same scene
played out in our kitchen: the lull before
the daily round of chores. The chairs, the tea,
the conversation – mum and our neighbour.

'A kitchen's the heart of a home', she'd say
as though quoting from Shakespeare. I never
thought to ask her where that came from, but day
after day, this rite was theirs together.

Of course, it couldn't last. The world moved on
with its wakes and partings; and yet it's strange.
Though many years have passed, it holds me still –
that simple heart of the home. Nothing's gone
from the scene; only the actors have changed.
It's our rite now. We have those roles to fill.

2008

Fitness Regime

Oh, what is the point of gymnasia?
You sign up in search of a dream:
to seek out the slim
in the way out of trim
when your senses weren't born to be lean.

Oh, what is the point of gymnasia?
You start with such noble intent:
to burn it away
during lunchtime each day,
but that craving you can't circumvent.

Oh, what is the point of gymnasia?
Your brain says your body must work.
You coughed up the dough
so your muscles must grow,
but the demon within wants to shirk.

Oh, what is the point of gymnasia?
Your membership's come round again.
Each year, you do less
to reduce this distress,
so you reach for your cheque book and pen ...

So, what is the point of gymnasia?
A way of assuaging your fear.
They cream off your cash
in a guilt-induced flash,
but expect not to see you this year.

Yes, they expect not to see you this year.

At least – not much.

2008

Ageing Eyes

Ever more time is lost to sleeping.
Focus gone and lens unbending,
ageing eyes are fixed on tending
faltering flowers. She is weeping.

The slow decline is never ending.
No more now the heart goes leaping.
Ageing eyes their watch are keeping
over the garden, comprehending.

2008, 2010

Vanishing Point

The hint of light that beckons from the west
reflects on tapered silver rails that gleam
into a vanishing point where I must go,
recalled by my day return from a dream.

It's quiet now and the station's at rest.
This is not Carnforth in the age of steam;
but the lingering, and the ebbing glow,
and our little silences, share a theme.

2008

Friesians

Aligned by the gently ticking wire,
these Friesians make a statement in mid-distance:
unmoving, bold, black and white daubs
deployed in a living sculpture
to permanence and belonging.

Time and again, I've seen that line.
Perhaps it's the August heat that stills them so.
Perhaps they are not real. Or perhaps
it's synchronous, and they simply appear
for everyman journeying here.

How long have the cattle owned this scene?
Since before this metalled road was laid,
when the farmer's cart skewed over
ruts and potholes, and the burnished back
of the mower felled his wheat.

The passing boatman must have seen them too.
Though his trade and canal have gone,
the cattle still keep watch – the sentinels
who first trod down his emptying waterway
and trampled it deep in the hungry clay.

2008

Ciara

For Heather, on losing her beloved Dutch rabbit

No small furry face peers out from the hutch.
No litter tray bangs in the dead of the night.
No hay manger rattles; no black and no white;
no sound and no movement; no beautiful Dutch.

Your glistening coat was so smooth to the touch.
Your mischievous eyes were so brimful of light.
Your company made the most wrong of days right.
You're suddenly gone; and I miss you so much.

I wish for a different world, where disease
could never lay claim to such innocent things;
but dust and decay are the fruits of this land.

Syringes of medicine, needles, vet's fees
foreshadowed this darkness; but still the loss stings –
this warm, loving life that was snatched from my hand.

2008

All That Matters

I see the tiredness in your eyes;
a missing glow. I recognise
the driven pace in my life too,
and half-resent the work we do.

The days can be a chore, I know.
'Life should be more.' Yet even so,
we have a gift; because we share
the solace of each other's care.

2008

Who Will Make the Water Clean?

Disease pollutes the river's flow.
Disease pollutes the stream.
Disease pollutes each standing pool.
Who can make the water clean?

Another world has everything.
Another world grows fat.
Another world cries 'Poverty!'
Who runs baths from silver taps?

The gift is such a simple thing,
so simple it's unseen;
the gift we turn to every day.
We can make the water clean.

2008

In a Garden

You were here too: inscrutable,
as usual; a man of few words.
By the fruit canes we stood,
where the ivy now grows
and the larch lap bends beneath
its burden of years.

I do not think of you often.
That analytical mind, with its quick
stratagems and formulae,
was unlike mine. Was there an
answer? A way through the woods?
I would never have asked had I known.

2008

Tyneham

*The Dorset village of Tyneham was evacuated
in 1943 with the promise, never kept, that the
villagers would return when peace was restored*

Five weeks before Christmas, the letters came;
from Southern Command. 'Make this sacrifice.
Give this help with a good heart.' Frost and ice
rimmed windows as the army staked its claim.

Six days before Christmas, the lorries came;
disorganised, late. They were rather few,
but with time tightening and the deadline due,
they drained the village to a haunted name.

I was sixteen when I first saw Tyneham's
gunnery-battered stones and broken bricks;
visible signs that war was still waged there.

It's sanitised now. Military wisdom's
prevailed. Tourists park up, hike, spread picnics,
but when they're gone, shells whistle through the air.

2008, 2009

The Unchanged Room

Its worn furniture softens this room.
Threadbare would speak of poverty,
maybe neglect. Pristine would say 'Pride'.
Only a room that's fussed over is pristine.

No genuine home glistens like that.
Who wouldn't praise care, discourage damage?
But something remains where a child's toy
clumsily hits the skirting board, or

the clasp on the dog's distressed lead
daily clinks on the hand-worn newel post.
In time to come, you'll sand away
these blemishes, then paint them out,

but each one shares the family history,
and as you place a singular brush stroke,
there'll come the recall, the fleeting memory
of some moment, some child now flown.

2009

Owencarrow Viaduct

To look at it now, you'd never think
that anything steel had passed this way.
Marsh grass and heather possess this low
gully of rock, and the dull Irish rain

has started a mire where peat will form
millennia hence. But look again:
the gully deepens. Its sides so straight,
deliberate and strong still betray

teams of navvies a century on.
To the north stand masonry arches
and a lone pier where Barnes Gap was spanned,
then the long curve to Owencarrow

where a viaduct crossed the valley,
high and wide, springing from a narrow
ledge and teetering slowly over
a tangle of river-fed marshes.

Grief and loss still permeate that place,
where a storm's blast toppled a carriage:
the roof couldn't hold, gave way, and poor
screaming souls fell from the raging sky.

Families knew that something was wrong:
the train not heard, the wind in full cry,
loved ones in the shallows. Then the twist
of tearing, tumbling, lethal wreckage.

2009

Tornado Torment

For Peter Treharne

Tornado torment,
a fearsome complaint.
It weakens my knees
and makes me feel faint.
Countless admirers
with homage to pay
question me senseless
and torture each day.

Tornado torment,
the queries cascade.
Sometimes I wish
it had never been made.

Tornado torment:
so where has it been?
Who bought each rivet
and why is it green?
When is it coming
and when will it go?
Where was it yesterday?
Why don't you know?

Tornado torment,
that engine again!
If only I'd something
to deaden the pain.

Tornado torment:
I've had it to here!
I'm through with inquisitors
bending my ear.
I'm closing the station
and lifting the track.
I'll make sure Tornado
can never come back.

Tornado torment,
there's nothing to lose.
I'm serving my notice
and taking to booze.

2009

Post-War Heaven

I registered the newness of it all –
the lawn-fringed high rise, regimented, neat –
long before I learned to read the fall
of bombs from infills in a London street.
We lived across the road, safe from that fate,
although a patch in a bedroom ceiling gave
away the point where a firebomb crashed straight
through the roof, and our terrace was saved
by a china doll, eiderdown, horse hair
mattress and bed springs that stopped it short
of detonation. They found it in mid air,
primed for destruction – but caught.

I was not there to know how personal
this made the war feel, but no one seemed
to rate it much. Mum cried for her broken doll,
but that stillborn bomb was life when death streamed
from the sky nightly. With the war gone,
a different foe changed the street forever:
housing policy moved the families on
who lived through it all, their new homes never
the same without the neighbours who shared
that common hell. Each soul was given
a precise amount of space; not one spared
a place in post-war heaven.

2009

Snagged

I start with a list of what needs to be done
but never quite get to the end of the page.
Distractions and tangents are so much more fun
than cold obligations, which soon disengage

that part of the brain which compels me to work.
Look! Here comes an email. Now what's that about?
I start out sincerely, not meaning to shirk,
but what my attention could most do without

are insights, diversions, beguiling ideas,
the time to pursue them, to see where they fly.
The bills are unpaid and the rent's in arrears,
and, yes – in all truth, it's not hard to see why.

I fear that I must be deficient in zeal
for facing life's cycle of everyday chores,
but duty will rapidly lose its appeal
to one who's averse to an errand that bores.

My feeble attention is flagging again.
My off-task antennae tune into the air
and random activity fires through my brain:
I'm snagged by a poem, but what do I care?

I start with a list of what needs to be done
but never quite get to the end of the page.
Distractions and tangents are so much more fun,
but so time-consuming. I *must* disengage!

2009, 2010

Catching the Train

It's a day of mist and drizzle,
like so many this May, but without
exception, they observe their routine –
late start, packed lunch, day out;

a pattern learned in childhood but still
an effective ruse for giving
the lie to that old question: 'Did you
have a good time?' It's the living

away from home that cheers them now:
damn the letters and damn the bills
two hundred miles away! They can rot
for a week. Outside, a damp breeze chills,

but they will not be deterred – they have
escaped, and this week is theirs, theirs
alone to do with as they choose, and
no dull meteorological cares

will bend them from their will. Agreed,
they set off for the station, only to find
that their timing's on holiday too,
and the parting train has left them behind.

He triggers the shutter; somehow catches
a scene as English as rain, distilled
in the lens: a plume of steam, wild flowers
in swathes, and distant misty hills.

2009

Relative Dangers

Rabbits line this crowded road,
but they are unafraid of cars
and browse the long, lush grass
(exhaust enriched with car-spray dressing)
that fronts the deadly tarmac.

Instruments of rabbit death
hurtle past, unseeing. None flinches
or inches away from the flattening
treads; but they shoot like rockets
at my approach – on a bike.

2009

The Gardener's Lament

Much of it seems futile.
This lawn is hardly grass.
Moss invades the greensward.
Yarrow never dies.

Molluscs ravage vegetables.
Birds impale the fruit.
Wind brings seed and spore in.
Weeds are on the rise.

Hope attends the planting.
What ails the tender shoots?
Aphid swarms have landed:
black, green, white flies.

2009

Collision Report

I saw the car before it hit;
a bolt of recognition.
Then it's blank – there's something missing.
The sky was clear, the moon bright,
and easy miles beckoned me on
through the warm September night.
His car didn't stop. Cue impact.
Later, blurted contrition.

I saw the car before it hit;
a half-sensed apparition,
this place, some weeks before, crazy,
banished, wild imagining.
The shock was the sudden dawning,
this was real and happening.
He looked right through me and drove on.
Cue cyclist demolition.

2009

Tinhale Barn, North Bersted

A lone barn stood here forty years ago:
brick and flint beneath a hipped roof,
its vast doors slouching in their frame.
The clay soil, worn by the few who passed,
bore fleeting prints: a cycle tyre, a hoof,
a plimsoll, a dog's paw; rare, unhurried traffic.
Below the broad Sussex sky, the ancient land
stretched fertile, ditch-drained and lush.

The barn's decline grew ever out of hand;
now it's gone. Weather, time, neglect, the slow
accretion of moss, all made it sick.
Crumbling mortar lost its hold at last,
and maybe bricks, flints, tiles fell. The hush
at the grave is expectant. Here's the stillness
before machines. The future's in harness.
Tinhale Road, Drive, Close. Choose its name.

2009, 2010

The Twelve Drays of Christmas

For David James

On the first dray of Christmas,
My true love sent to me
A firkin of golden draught beer.

On the second dray of Christmas,
My true love sent to me
Two yards of ale,
And a firkin of golden draught beer.

On the third dray of Christmas,
My true love sent to me
Three packs of ice,
Two yards of ale,
And a firkin of golden draught beer.

On the fourth dray of Christmas,
My true love sent to me
Four barley wines,
Three packs of ice,
Two yards of ale,
And a firkin of golden draught beer.

On the fifth dray of Christmas,
My true love sent to me
Five Highland malts,
Four barley wines,
Three packs of ice,
Two yards of ale,
And a firkin of golden draught beer.

On the sixth dray of Christmas,
My true love sent to me
Six Alka-Seltzers,
Five Highland malts,
Four barley wines,
Three packs of ice,
Two yards of ale,
And a firkin of golden draught beer.

On the seventh dray of Christmas,
My true love sent to me
Seven casks of bitter,
Six Alka-Seltzers,
Five Highland malts,
Four barley wines,
Three packs of ice,
Two yards of ale,
And a firkin of golden draught beer.

On the eighth dray of Christmas,
My true love sent to me
Eight kegs of Guinness,
Seven casks of bitter,
Six Alka-Seltzers,
Five Highland malts,
Four barley wines,
Three packs of ice,
Two yards of ale,
And a firkin of golden draught beer.

On the ninth dray of Christmas,
My true love sent to me
Nine tins of Andrews,
Eight kegs of Guinness,
Seven casks of bitter,
Six Alka-Seltzers,
Five Highland malts,
Four barley wines,
Three packs of ice,
Two yards of ale,
And a firkin of golden draught beer.

On the tenth dray of Christmas,
My true love sent to me
Ten tuns of porter,
Nine tins of Andrews,
Eight kegs of Guinness,
Seven casks of bitter,
Six Alka-Seltzers,
Five Highland malts,
Four barley wines,

Three packs of ice,
Two yards of ale,
And a firkin of golden draught beer.

On the eleventh dray of Christmas,
My true love sent to me
Eleven Irish whiskeys,
Ten tuns of porter,
Nine tins of Andrews,
Eight kegs of Guinness,
Seven casks of bitter,
Six Alka-Seltzers,
Five Highland malts,
Four barley wines,
Three packs of ice,
Two yards of ale,
And a firkin of golden draught beer.

On the twelfth dray of Christmas,
My true love sent to me
Twelve paramedics,
Eleven Irish whiskeys,
Ten tuns of porter,
Nine tins of Andrews,
Eight kegs of Guinness,
Seven casks of bitter,
Six Alka-Seltzers,
Five Highland malts,
Four barley wines,
Three packs of ice,
Two yards of ale,
And a firkin of golden draught beer.

2009

Leaving Ireland

October 2005

The mountains rise to meet the crowded sky.
Beneath its leaden sheets, the rain drives down
the grasses and the tussocks of wet moss.
The oranges and greens, and greys and browns,
compose a sodden sketch beyond the screen.
The wipers swish, the tyres throw sheets of spray
as onwards, ever onwards, we ship out,
all mute, all knowing this, our final day,
will end upon a car deck of wet steel.

Through slow and narrow lanes, we let the thread
of this last journey weave a lasting spell.
The straining crowds choose faster roads and head
to Cobh for souvenirs, where they will wait,
grow bored and tarnish new-formed memories.
Instead, we take the winding, idle way
in this unhurried land to say goodbye.

2009, 2010

Making Space

The study's shelves now groan. Their serried ranks
demand a cull. But what should stay, or go?
So many books, so few without a cause.
A section filled with guides to beer. A shelf
of maps (well thumbed). And railway stuff in spades,
a photographic catalogue of change.
And loss. *Per ardua ad nulla* – all
for nought; enough to raise a navvy's ire,
the thought that some fat bureaucrat could scrub
his life's work out. The waterways, against
the odds, survive because of holidays,
when boating types frequent their locks and bars.
They claim a shelf. Then poetry, and next
some works of reference. Novels? Just a few.

Computer books. Now there are words to doubt;
the verbiage of driven change. Rolling
upgrades, streaming night and day, claim to keep
my PC safe from harm. It must reboot
but now it crawls, as tardy as a three-
toed sloth. Perhaps I ought to change my tack
and scrap the hapless thing? I'd have some space
and might get by with pen and ink. But no,
it has me hooked. I'd struggle now to write
my verse by hand – a turncoat through and through.
Mind you, I'll ditch the manuals. They don't
describe this dire morass of software now.
Unloved, unread and unto death they go:
the failsafe, pain-free way of making space.

2009

Reaction Lift

Reaction lift induces flight.
And so with love. No other ride
so redefines us, warms us, thrills,
embraces, casts old cares aside.

You found me at a time when I
was mired in listless, numb routine.
It fell apart. And I must start
to learn again what life can mean.

2010

Conundrum

The clanking army cleverly spurned all clay *en route,*
choosing chaste downland chalk for its conquering roads.
Neither mire nor morass beset them as they marched to claim
the fecund rural riches of ragged native tribes.

Across the south, Rome's sudden, sweeping tide
brought fear and flight – or fortune for client kings.
Near Dorchester, the stubborn Durotriges dug in.
Ballista bolts soon brought the message home:
succumb or be slaughtered. Choose servitude for life.

How could this have heralded four hundred years of peace?

2010

Through a Window

The scene recalls a snow globe:
flakes swirling to earth
enchant as rain never can.
Winter spreads her girth.

The broken, hunch-backed garden,
buds and blooms long past,
slowly grows smooth and shapeless;
a ruin recast.

Although the season's future
holds grime, thaw and mire,
for now the speckled window
reflects the hearth's fire

and all is right with the world:
fresh-laid snow outside;
the thought that routine will stall,
thanks to this, inside.

2010

The Ballad of Transport Paralysis

In Sussex, there's a dismal town
whose roads are full of holes,
the envy of mad rabbit gangs,
of badgers and of moles.

The excavators come unseen
by cover of the night,
when every woman, man and child
retreats in hasty flight.

They dig 'em deep and dig 'em wide
through chalk and clay and loam,
but just before the dawn arrives,
the diggers head for home.

They mark their work with traffic lights
and some unused machine,
while serried ranks of plastic cones
add colour to the scene.

No labourers assemble there,
no foreman stands in charge,
no clipboard-waving manager;
there's not a soul at large ...

And yet these holes possess the place –
along with traffic queues,
and gently fuming motorists
all tuned in to the news

that gridlock has returned to town,
their journeys are in vain,
and now the bloody useless holes
are filling up with rain,

so if some tarmac-laying man
should visit them today,
he'll have a ready-made excuse
to turn and go away.

2010

A Final Poem

A final poem
should be a sombre thing,
possessed of *gravitas*
and self-knowledge.

It should know what to do
in an emergency,
be confident, a good public speaker,
able to hold its liquor.

It should be eloquent, versatile,
poised to speak at any moment
on any subject – life, death, mysteries,
the prices they charge in the shops –

a comfort in time of trouble,
faithful friend, strong staff,
the question, the answer,
sympathiser, antagonist.

A really good final poem
knows when to stop,
doesn't go on,
never becomes a bore.

Yes. This might do.

2010

Notes

In 2007, I was found to have a serious heart problem which took 2½ years to diagnose. Barely four months after this was brought under control, I was run down on my bicycle by a motorist and thought at the moment of impact that my end had come. Luckily it had not, but six months on from this calamity it seemed wise to make a permanent record of my writing in case anything else befell me. In compiling this collection, I re-visited every piece of verse which I felt had merit and, where necessary, carried out more 'hammering into shape'. The results must speak for themselves, but these notes provide background information where I felt that this would help.

The Castle (1969). Corfe Castle in Dorset was once used by King John to store 50,000 marks from his royal treasury. During the Civil War, it was besieged by Parliamentary forces but Lady Mary Bankes, wife of the absent owner, organised a scratch garrison of merchants and villagers to defend it. The siege was broken in February 1646, when the defenders were tricked into admitting supposed reinforcements. The following month, the castle was 'slighted', i.e. made unusable, by order of Parliament.

Promises, Promises (1975). Several social and political documentaries on television reminded me that this lyric was written at a time of great unrest in the UK. The country was in turmoil: under attack by the IRA, struggling with high inflation, and crippled by strikes. Politicians promising a better future were an easy target, and I took a shot. Years later, the age of political 'spin' encouraged me to update the lyric for a new outing. The music recorded in 1975 began with the short invented speech at the end of this paragraph, although it must be conceded that modern politicians no longer speak in these terms, even in satire. The speaker was gradually drowned out by guitar, bass and drums, which – in hindsight – seems an appropriate metaphor for the whole turbulent time. This is what he intoned: 'The social, economic and moral problems facing this country are not incurable, as the pessimists suppose. We are living in a highly sophisticated society, not in mediaeval tutelage to our social superiors; and the answers that we find to the problems of today will guide posterity to a better future.' Are we there yet?

Michael Otto (1975). My parents acted as 'host family' to a number of young German students during the mid 1970s. Michael Otto, 11 or 12 at the time, was the most energetic of them. He is probably now a wealthy businessman.

The Quest (1976). This lyric, with its deliberately boring rhyme scheme (aaaa, bbbb, etc.), was intended to be a pastiche of a folk song, written partly to lambaste the gassy, processed keg beer of the 1970s. However, it was so successful in this aim that many assumed it to be the 'real thing', imagining, perhaps, that bygone farm workers had composed this beery eulogy (originally in honour of Portsmouth-brewed 'Gales Ales') after a hard day's labour in the fields. The lyric started life as 'The HSB Song', named after Horndean Special Bitter which was the company's flagship product, developed in 1959 by then head brewer Ted Argyle. However, the family owners sold up in 2005, and the buyers closed their historic brewery permanently from 1st April 2006. There is no point in having a drinking song based on a brewery that no longer exists, so the piece was extended and re-worked to celebrate ASB, or Arundel Special Bitter, which is produced by the new Arundel Brewery.

Nails (1977). *Pax Romana* is Latin for 'the Roman peace', i.e. 400 years' peace, or near peace, under Roman rule; *inhumana* means 'cruel, barbarous, inhuman' *(Cassell's Compact Latin Dictionary)*.

The Garbage Lives (1982). 'Beaufort' refers to the Beaufort scale of wind speeds, developed by Sir Francis Beaufort in 1805. It seems to be little used in inland weather forecasts, except when the wind is expected to reach force 8 or above; but these were the speeds attained on this occasion in Southampton.

Turl Street (1984). I do not suppose that the city fathers of Oxford will like this poem very much but, when I visited the city over a sultry weekend in July 1984, parts of it were not exactly edifying to behold. Unfortunately for the city fathers, these sights made more of an impression on me than the dreaming spires. (Hopefully, Saturday-night Oxford has cleaned up its act in the intervening years.) In a rant against urban filth, I have parodied a line from Blake's 'Jerusalem' and several phrases from John of Gaunt's famous speech in Shakespeare's 'Richard II'.

A Cornish Lament (1985). In his verse autobiography, *Summoned By Bells,* John Betjeman provides an evocative description of a train journey from Waterloo to Wadebridge by way of the scenic North Cornwall line. The route was closed in October 1966, with Barbara Castle – then Minister of State for Transport – attracting some of the opprobrium for the loss, rather than Dr. Richard Beeching whose

1963 report, *The Reshaping of British Railways,* had included it in a long list of lines to be axed. Dr. Beeching's report had been published under a Conservative administration but, when Labour won the 1964 general election, locals had hoped that Mrs. Castle would halt the closures – in vain, as it turned out. Nearly twenty years after the axe fell, the North Cornwall line presented a forlorn sight.

Hard Times and Rotten Rhymes (1985). In 1985, Faber & Faber published an anthology of northern verse entitled *Hard Lines.* A contributor was interviewed on Radio 4, but his vision of England seemed to be based on the premise that most people living in the south of the country were wealthy, materialistic and egotistical. The culture of greed engendered by the Thatcher government no doubt helped to shape this view, but for many southerners – especially those not born with a silver spoon in their mouth – the poems may have sounded sour, superficial and even tiresome.

Wedgwood Blues (1985). Barlaston is the home of the Wedgwood factory shop, which I visited when cruising along the Trent & Mersey Canal in a narrowboat. The prices for dinner services ranged up to £1,543, which seems stratospheric even now, 35 years later. American tourists quizzed the sales staff as to whether or not the products were dishwasher-proof. (It would not do to have the gilt washed down the waste pipe.) I suspect that most Britons would treat such a purchase as an investment and never use it.

On Spetisbury Station, Dorset (1986). The name is pronounced 'Spetsbry'. Denis Baxter's oil painting of the abandoned and overgrown station steps was entitled, 'There'll be no more a-rushin' to catch the Spetisbury train', and it is from the title that this vignette was formed. Denis's wonderfully atmospheric painting was sold to a private collector, which, sadly, has ensured that it remains unknown.

Art (1997). An experienced computer programmer can write hundreds of lines of program code every day, but only a machine will ever 'read' his work regularly.

Cleeve Abbey (1998). Cleeve Abbey, Somerset, was a Cistercian foundation dissolved by Henry VIII in 1536. After the dissolution, it was used as a farm with some of the smaller ground floor rooms serving as stables. Part of the cloister was converted into a kitchen.

While grander abbeys became stately homes (often much altered), the humble inheritance of Cleeve enabled it to survive largely intact for over four centuries, until its value was recognised. In 1950, it was sold to the Commissioners of Crown Lands, who transferred it a year later to the Ministry of Works. Since 1984, the abbey has been in the care of English Heritage.

Stogumber Station (2001). This is a rustic halt on the branch line from Taunton to Minehead, now preserved by the West Somerset Railway. The cantilevered wooden platform perches above the surrounding valley, but few rooftops can be seen since the village it serves lies a mile to the west, at the top of a steep hill. The old fashioned lanterns are reproductions, made by an enthusiast who studied Victorian photographs to establish the design of the originals. These lanterns now house long life light bulbs rather than oil lamps – a concession to modern concerns about economics and ecology – but the effect of the whole is very convincing, and offers instant time travel back to about 1950.

Powerstock (2002). I consider myself fortunate to have travelled often on the former railway from Maiden Newton to Bridport, through scenery and places that belonged more to the time of Thomas Hardy than the modern world, accompanied by the Dorset burr of country wives travelling to market with their empty baskets. Closed in May 1975, the trackbed survives as a gently etched line through the landscape – part farm track, part footpath, part thicket and scrub. Powerstock was the second station along the branch and, like Stogumber (see above), remote from the village it served, although this time the natural obstacle in between was a deep valley rather than a steep hill. With such a demanding walk to the station, bygone passengers must have been fit, but cars lured them all away, and then scrap metal men tore up the rails. Now the station slumbers in quiet solitude, disturbed only by passing foxes and gulls. A few pubs survive in this remote area, but they cater mainly for diners, and scrubbed tables are a thing of the past.

The Winchester Diver (2002). Winchester Cathedral was constructed on a raft of large beechwood logs, which, by 1900, was disintegrating and threatening the cathedral with collapse. Between 1906 and 1911, during a comprehensive restoration project, the diver William Walker underpinned the walls with concrete, spending 6 hours a day in a black liquid 'soup' in which he had to work by touch alone. Centuries earlier, the stained glass windows at the west end were destroyed during the Civil War, but worshippers saved the fragments so that a new window could be fashioned from pieces of the old. King George V's words, quoted at the head of the poem, come from the cathedral's service of re-dedication in 1912.

I'll Never Be Romantic (2005). Lord Byron's ancestral home was Newstead Abbey, where he threw a number of extravagant and excessive parties. To this day, the building contains bullet holes from his pistol practice, which he directed at the walls of the roofless refectory. He would have kept modern reporters in work for years.

Getting in the Stride (2007). Stride is a style of jazz piano playing which originated in Harlem in 1919, and was popular during the 1930s and 1940s. It was influenced partly by ragtime, but also included improvisation, blue notes and swing rhythms. Thomas Wright Waller, who lived from 1904 to 1943, was considered to be the best stride player of his time. The son of an American Baptist minister, Thomas acquired his love of the organ and piano as a lad at church; but he is known to history as 'Fats' Waller. My father was an accomplished player of his music.

The Fall and Rise of St. George (2007). This piece was written for a St. George's Day concert. On 2nd June 1893, Pope Leo XIII replaced St. George with St. Peter as Patron Saint of England, and relegated St. George to 'national protector' (a secondary role). A further demotion occurred in 1963, when St. George was reduced to a third class minor saint and removed from the Universal Church Calendar. Worse followed in 1969, when his feast day (23rd April) was reduced to an optional memorial in the Calendar, its solemnity depending on local observance. The tide turned in 2000, when Pope John Paul II restored St. George to the Calendar, and, since then, he has appeared in Missals as the Patron Saint of England, with Pope Leo's changes ignored. It was probably a coincidence that Pope John Paul's decision followed the passing in 1998 of the Scotland Act and the Government of Wales Act, which devolved varying amounts of power from Westminster to Edinburgh and Cardiff. One by-product of devolution has been the increasing use in England of St. George's flag when, previously, the Union flag would have been used.

Deluge (2007). In the summer of 2007, the UK was hit by sustained heavy rainfall and the worst flooding for decades. While Sussex escaped relatively lightly compared with other parts of the country, it was a dire season that brought disaster in its wake – quite literally.

Hedgehog Duty (2007). 'ĕrĭnā´ceous (-shus), adj. Of the hedgehog family; like, or characteristic of, a hedgehog. From the Latin *erinaceus*, hedgehog.' (Webster's Online Dictionary)

Light Pollution (2007). 'Shine on, sodium!' Most street lights are sodium vapour lights, which are used because the yellow/orange light given off is close to the maximum sensitivity of the human eye.

Vanishing Point (2008). Carnforth was the Lancashire railway station where David Lean filmed 'Brief Encounter'.

Friesians (2008). Friesians are the famous breed of black and white cattle introduced into England during the 17th and 18th centuries. The 'mower' referred to in line 15 is an agricultural labourer, who felled hay, wheat, barley, etc. with a sickle. Such a labourer is the principal character in 'The Mower', a short story by H.E. Bates which recalls a scene that he must have witnessed as a boy in the early years of the 20th century.

Ciara (2008). The Dutch rabbit is one of the oldest breeds of pet rabbit. The animals have a distinctive band of white fur around their chest, which continues up the neck, over the nose and on to the forehead; the rest of their fur is black, grey, brown or amber. Ciara was a classic black and white Dutch.

Who Will Make the Water Clean? (2008). 'Another world cries "Poverty!"' By the end of 2008, the so-called 'credit crunch' had led to considerable economic disruption in the west, but poverty is relative.

In a Garden (2008). Larch lap is a type of fencing, with strips of larch woven alternately over and under vertical struts. 'The Way Through the Woods' is a poem by Rudyard Kipling.

Owencarrow Viaduct (2009). This poem refers to a major tragedy in Irish railway history which occurred in the remote countryside of County Donegal. On Friday 30th January 1925, winds calculated to have been gusting at up to 120 m.p.h. blew the first carriage of the 7 p.m. Letterkenny to Burtonport train off of

Owencarrow Viaduct. The viaduct was situated just north of Barnes Gap, three miles before the next station at Creeslough – which is how far fireman John Hannigan had to walk, through appalling conditions, to summon help. Given the ferocity of the weather, it is miraculous that only one carriage was derailed and only four passengers killed.

Tornado Torment (2009). From 1992 to 2010, Peter Treharne was station master at Blue Anchor on the preserved West Somerset Railway, which the 2008-built steam locomotive 'Tornado' visited in May and June 2009. To describe the public's reaction to the visit as enthusiastic is an understatement, as witnessed by their mantra in the week leading up to the engine's arrival: 'When is Tornado coming?' Subsequent questions were the tricky ones, for some of them verged on sub-atomic detail. It was an odd experience to supply the same information so many times, and unusual to be able to predict the question, or even answer it before it had been asked. The week felt like a succession of scenes from the film 'Groundhog Day', a comedy starring Bill Murray, in which an irascible weather reporter is trapped in recurrences of the same day. The lyric is also a parody of 'Typewriter Torment' by Keith Reid, who is best known as the 'poet in residence' with rock band Procol Harum.

The Twelve Drays of Christmas (2009). This is a frivolous piece that my friend David James put me up to over a pint in The Maypole Inn at Yapton, hence the dedication. A firkin is a cask containing 9 gallons of beer, while its larger relative, the tun, contains 216 gallons. A yard of ale is a very tall glass with a large bulb at the end, often used in ale-drinking competitions. The drinker has to be skilled (and fairly sober) to prevent the contents of the bulb gushing out at once as the glass is drained. The reference to 'Andrews' is shorthand for 'Andrews Liver Salts', which have been described as the 'Rolls Royce of hangover cures'. This lyric is not 'politically correct' but, as anyone with a grain of sense will realise, it is hyperbolic and does not describe a recommended liquid diet.

Leaving Ireland (2009). The oranges and greens referred to are the autumn colours of the peat bogs in County Kerry rather than the colours of the Irish flag. Cobh is pronounced 'Cove' and was formerly Queenstown, the Irish port where RMS Titanic made her final call in April 1912 before setting off on her fateful journey across the Atlantic.

Making Space (2009).   This was written as an exercise using iambic pentameters. *Per ardua ad nulla* is a misquote of the RAF's motto, *Per ardua ad astra,* which means 'Through adversity to the stars'. This variation means 'Through adversity to ruins' (literally 'nothings'). The 'u' in *'nulla'* is pronounced as in 'pull'. The 'ruins' or 'nothings' refer to Dr. Richard Beeching's government-inspired 're-shaping' of the nation's rail network in the 1960s, which for many communities was a euphemism for 'closing'.

Conundrum (2010). This piece takes its cue from Saxon poetry, with four heavy stresses in each line, the first three being alliterative. However, I suspect that my lines contain too many syllables for 'Conundrum' to be a fully convincing example of the genre. There is also something slightly suspect in my 'historical timing', since Saxon poetry reached these islands as the Romans withdrew rather than when they arrived.

Sources. These notes were compiled largely from memory, often based on personal experience, but websites belonging to organisations such as Wikipedia, the National Trust, the University of Bath (very good on the lost village of Tyneham) and The Irish Times were used to confirm the historical details referred to in some of the poems.   Since Wikipedia has an 'open editing' policy, information from this source was verified elsewhere. The following publications were also consulted:

- Bussby, Frederick, *William Walker: The Diver Who Saved Winchester Cathedral,* 1994, Friends of Winchester Cathedral, ISBN 0 903346 16 8
- Gilyard-Beer, R., *Cleeve Abbey,* 1998, English Heritage, ISBN 1 85074 280 4
- Wright, Patrick, *The Village That Died For England,* 2002, Faber & Faber, ISBN 0 571 21441 X

If any errors remain in the factual content of my historical poems, then the fault is entirely mine and I will be pleased to receive corrections via the publisher.